TOWARD THE RIGHT ROAD

Berdie Gehring

With Charlotte Garrick

World rights reserved. This book or any portion thereof may not be copied or reproduced in any form or manner whatever, except as provided by law, without the written permission of the publisher, except by a reviewer who may quote brief passages in a review.

The author assumes full responsibility for the accuracy of all facts and quotations as cited in this book. The opinions expressed in this book are the author's personal views and interpretations, and do not necessarily reflect those of the publisher.

This book is provided with the understanding that the publisher is not engaged in giving spiritual, legal, medical, or other professional advice. If authoritative advice is needed, the reader should seek the counsel of a competent professional.

Copyright © 2021 Berdie Gehring
Copyright © 2021 TEACH Services, Inc.
ISBN-13: 978-1-4796-1226-0 (Paperback)
ISBN-13: 978-1-4796-1227-7 (ePub)
Library of Congress Control Number: 2020920228

All Bible references are taken from the King James Version (KJV) of the Bible. Public domain.

Published by

Two Streets

Matthew 7:13, 14

The lights sparkle brightly
In the dark of the night;
The millions who walk there
Are dazzled by the sight.
It is the street, broad way.

Some souls stumble onward
As new pleasures they seek
In palaces on thiw way
Where thrills reach their peak.
It is the street, broad way.

Others are funning wildly
In fits of ecstasy;
While some race on endlessly
To some imagined rhapsody.
It is the street, broad way.

To end of this street so wide
Always in contruction
Of things to deceive th lost;
This way to hell and desctruction.
It is the street, broad way.

If one chooses to change direction
On this road to deception,
He'll discover a strange phenomenon,
That this same street he is on
Is now called Narrow Way!

—Charlotte Garrick

Table of Contents

Foreword . . . . *ix*

Chapter One **10**
   His Name Was Verl. 11
   Verl Again? 20

Chapter Two. **21**
   Three Silver Bullets 21

Chapter Three **31**
   The Potato Room .31

Chapter Four **37**
   The Safety Net 37
   Wild Child 39
   Ice Ahead. 40
   Betty Jo 42
   Dry Tank 43
   A New Daddy. 43

Chapter Five **46**
   The Turnaround 46
   The House Rules. 48
   Facing the Judge 52

Chapter Six **56**
   Brand New 56
   The Sabbath?. 57
   Freedom 58
   In Transition 59

Chapter Seven **61**
   Breaking Home Ties. 61
   Pigs?. 63
   Finally, a Motorcycle! 64

Chapter Eight **69**
   An Interesting Encounter 69
   Back on the Streets. 71
   The Back Stroke? 74
   Graduation. 75

Chapter Nine **78**
   Mistaken Identity. 78
   Pikes Peak. 84

Chapter Ten **87**
   Jail Houses Again 87
   About Mom. 89
   About Herb. 89
   Arizona 90

Chapter Eleven **92**
   High Noon 92
   The Wedding Day 97
   It's Snowing! 98
   I Am Praying for You 102
   What Happened to the Big, Blue House? 103

Chapter Twelve **106**
   Looking for a Church 106
   The Dreams. 110

Epilogue *118*

Foreword

Berdie Gehring writes graphically to help the reader picture the scences. This book is full of unbelievable but true stories. It would make an amazing movie! The story was written as related to Berdie. It tells how God leads in spite of some terrible situations. Never give up! God will see you through. Your life will seem wonderful compared to this story. You will find great faith that God can see you through anything. He loves and cares for you!

—Pastor Bill Waters, Jr.

Chapter One

———◆———

It seems that artists when painting a landscape will often put in a path or a road to show the viewer the way in or the way out of the scene. This is done in an effort to cast a feeling of peace over the painting, showing there is an avenue to elsewhere. That makes sense when viewed in the light of life's journey each day to another time and place ... the hope of heaven. Fifty some years ago I was thrust out into my own landscape of living only to find later that the way out was going to be tough going.

My first venture outside of my parents' house was not to church to hear the name of Jesus as some privileged children got to do. It was probably to a mall or to some friend's home. To be conscious of the existence of God would dawn fifteen years later upon my dark mind. The precious thought now is to know that God was aware of my presence in His world all through those years of being in a wilderness—a wilderness that was barren of His Word or any personal knowledge of Him. What feelings of love in the contemplation of the glorious truth that I was all the time in His care.

Telling my story has never been easy. Each time that I recall scene after scene from my memory, it opens wounds and scars that will probably never completely heal. I decided long ago that if it would help young and old alike to become aware of God and His great mercy I would tell it again and again. In my story I allude to some events more than once. Remember that. Since my conversion as a teenager, I've shared my story the world over. From audiences throughout the United States, to a tour in Israel, and an enthusiastic village audiences in Mexico, many have been privy to my account of salvation. It always ends with "Jesus in my heart" and an appeal for "Jesus in your heart, too." Just know and consider that as you read on.

His Name Was Verl

The first few years were uneventful except for the usual childhood diseases and mishaps around the house. Did I say uneventful? The truth is, as I go back into the years, that it was an awful start for a little girl to endure. My dad, who I just refer to as "Verl," was a wicked man, especially when he was drunk. He was very tall at 6' 6" and weighed around two hundred and sixty-five pounds, and I distinctly remember his round belly. Can you believe that?

The following may sound like fiction, however, it is true. Because of stress, I suppose, my potty training was slow. One day when I didn't perform, Verl put my head down in the commode and pushed the flush bar. For the same reason as above, I have cigarette-burn scars on my right arm and back. Really I do! Early in life, my tonsils became diseased and certainly needed to be surgically removed. And as a result of that surgery, I was not very energetic.

One day I was feeling so poorly that I curled up in Verl's chair to take a nap. That was a bad move on my part. When he came in from work in a drunken stupor and saw me in his chair, he screamed at me, "What are you doing in my chair?" He proceeded to pick me up and sling me across the room. Many times he beat me, his little girl, with the buckle end of his belt. And I could never understand why he didn't love me.

(The beatings with the belt were to stay with me. Later on, when I was around seventeen, I was visiting at a friend's house and someone had a belt in his hand. I saw the belt, and suddenly, without warning, I fell to the floor under the dining room table, and I cowered in an almost fetal position.

My hands were on my head, and I was screaming, "Please! Don't hit me! Don't hit me!" I must have had a flashback of memory, because I came back into the present with my friends over me saying, "Berdie, we aren't going to hit you. What's wrong?" And I told them as I am telling you now.)

Because of Verl's temperament, my little mother was put through unbelievable pain at times. I clearly remember the time that Mom got new glasses, and the ear pieces were hurting her ears. She complained of the pain, and just then Verl went over and clamped his hands down on her ears as hard as he could. Mom screamed, and he backed away. But then she did a remarkable thing for her size: She grabbed an iron skillet and hit Verl on his head two or three times as hard as she could. He yelled in pain as he staggered backward—first of all, because he was drunk, and second, because of Mom's banging on his head. It is humorous as I recall that now because he exclaimed in a drunken sort of way, "Well! That oughta knock some sense into me!" On he reeled back and forth as he went out the back door complaining of a headache.

The majority of time Verl got the best of Mom, and we all lived in terror from one day to the next. But where was she to go? What could she do? Uneducated. No money. Where would she have gone? There were no known facilities in our area at that time for battered women (or children). We were in a prison from which there seemed to be no relief and no hope.

Time wore on. Trouble was a constant visitor in our house, and finally Verl and Mom were divorced. Mom couldn't take it anymore. That was when a new "Daddy" came into my life. His name was Joseph, but I called him "Daddy." Joseph and his wife were friends of our family, but something happened to their marriage, and they were divorced. So Mom and Joseph were married at a later date, and we became a blended family of seven.

> *The majority of time Verl got the best of Mom, and we all lived in terror from one day to the next.*

Patrick, Joseph's oldest son, made the biggest impression on me as a child. I think it was because he was twelve years older than I. Joseph wore the name "Daddy" well. He declared that he loved me which made me so happy. My given name is Berdine, however, early on my family shortened that to just "Berdie." But Daddy decided that I would be known to him by the nicknames that he gave me—"Skinflint" and "Morning Glory." Both names were affectionately applied. I was Morning Glory when he said that I "brightened up a room" when I walked in. And Skinflint was for everyday use in conversation with skinny me. Finally I had a daddy who loved me—a little eight-year-old, scrawny, bony, pigeon-toed girl.

At some point, because of the deformity in my feet, my next older brother, Herb, thought of a practical way to straighten my feet which had been turned in from birth. By the time I was eight, this was causing me much discomfort as I tried to run and play with him. Even at his young age of twelve, he thought of a solution to correct my deformed feet. He decided to wrap them in gauze and then bind my ankles with plain old duck tape. Mom thought this was a very good idea and gave her approval to try this.

Each night he and Mom would wrap my ankles tightly to pull those joints outward. This seemed to help align my feet properly. Back then people weren't so educated to take their children to an orthopedic doctor or a podiatrist, yet this home-styled method did produce visible results. And then there was the problem of money. In addition to my misshapen feet, another source of discomfort was the narrow bite that I had and the deformity in the roof of my mouth. Some words were difficult for me as the result of this impairment. Because of this, I have endured some relentless teasing by this one and that one wherever

I went. But early on I realized that I was going to have some pretty tough struggles ahead to level things out and be able to function as others.

During this period of my life the doctors discovered that Mom had uterine cancer, and she spent time in the hospital and at home in recuperation. She was very sick after the surgery, and her confinement lasted almost three years. Since she was mostly bedridden, and I was the only other female in the house, it became my lot to step up at the young age of nine and grow up very fast.

I remember the day and the very words that forever changed my life. An old picnic table, which sat out under a certain big tree, served as a conference table for Daddy and me when we needed to talk. I always felt special that Daddy would discuss things with me—his childhood and military service, his children by two previous wives, sometimes little me, and now, Mom and her illness. He sank into that almost melancholy mood—I could sense something very important was about to be announced.

Finally, Daddy matter-of-factly said, "Skinflint, listen, honey. You are going to help me with the work." He must have noticed the bewildered look on my face because he came over and put his arm around my waist in a gesture of comfort. I know that he felt terrible at interrupting my childhood, but it was desperation on his part. He needed help.

Daddy produced a list of daily chores for me that he expected to be finished by the time he came home each evening. I'll never forget the time that I forgot one thing on the list. I was upstairs in my room looking for a toy or a coloring book and enjoying the quietness of the moment when I heard his voice at the bottom of the stairs. "Berdine, come down at once." Not Skinflint. Not Morning Glory. It was "Berdine…." I went down at lightning speed.

"Why did you skip the dusting?"

"I forgot."

"What do you mean, 'I forgot?'"

"I forgot."

"Okay. Come with me, young lady."

That was one of the few spankings that I ever needed from Daddy. He set the standard for me, and I learned really fast.

Daddy finally taught me how to starch some of our clothes—but not his service pants and not his handkerchiefs! He thought it was very amusing that I had starched his handkerchiefs so that they would stand up on one corner. He was a sharp dresser, as they say, and he was very particular about how he presented himself to the world each day.

Underneath his sometimes-stern exterior was a gentle spirit. He loved to help distribute food boxes to the needy around our town, and it was my joy to accompany him on these rounds of mercy. He very wisely considered Mom's health and my physical disadvantages in protecting myself—especially when he was away—and he set about to remedy that.

He started me on a program of exercise which included high jumping, calisthenics, and boxing. For a skinny kid, I became very strong and very adept at some karate moves that he had incorporated into the boxing routine. Boy-o-boy! That did wonders for my self-esteem at home and at school. Daddy, himself, was a boxer, and in moments of "horsing around" with me, he would hold my head in a headlock and vigorously rub the top of my head.

> *The old saying that "the sun rises and sets" in a person applied to my daddy. I stood in awe of the man, and I loved him. He was my protector, my teacher, and my daddy.*

I was a devoted pal of his. He taught me about motors, tools, and any other thing that he thought might aid me in my development. The old saying that "the sun rises and sets" in a person applied to my daddy. I stood in awe of the man, and I loved him. He was my protector, my teacher, and my daddy. He could do no wrong as far as I was concerned. He told me over and over that he loved me. I was devoted to him and to his every directive in my young life. Another thing that I thoroughly enjoyed was our trip to town each week for a steak for each of us. Perhaps it was the stress of Mom's illness. Or was it work? I don't know, but one day Daddy had a heart attack. This was disabling for a man who had been strong and independent. Now he had to slow down and let his body recuperate. He was sick, and he needed me; I would muster my strength, be a big girl, and always help him. He was my hero.

To my duties was added the responsibility of paying the bills. I wrote the checks, and Daddy signed them. I took them to the proper places such as the power company and the city offices for the water bill. Life was coming at me fast and furiously. I always tried to do my very best that was possible considering my age. Much was asked of me. Looking back as an adult, I'm sure there were many mistakes that were simply overlooked because of my young age. I had no time to fool around and get into trouble because I was busy at home and at school. I now believe with all my heart that God in His mercy was looking out for me. It had to be that. Perhaps there was an angel who was ever by my side. It had to be of the Lord's doing.

Verl Again?

Verl was constantly making vile threats that he would kidnap Herb and me; therefore, through the years we lived in different homes in different places. I remember one time that he and my daddy (Joseph) had a confrontation. It was an almost unbearable, sweltering hot day and tempers were boiling to overflowing. Daddy had a switchblade knife that he carried at the time, and I could see that he was going to use it on Verl. However, as dangerous as it was, I stepped between them begging, "Don't do this. It is not worth your going to prison." Instead, Daddy gave Verl a left/right uppercut which caused him to stagger backwards toward his car. His car window was down, and Daddy stuffed him, headfirst, into the window and sent him on his way.

This moving around meant changing schools a lot and leaving behind classmates and friends. Looking back, I think God was slowly preparing me to adjust to new situations and people for the time when I would reach adulthood. Of course God could see far into the future, and He knew exactly what I would need to be and do for His service. I couldn't see it then, but some events that would be life changing loomed on the distant horizon for me. Nothing prepared me for them.

Chapter Two

Three Silver Bullets

Mom had regained most of her strength by the time I turned twelve. It seemed so good having her back in the kitchen preparing gourmet meals for which she became famous. I could relax a bit and enjoy growing up, although I thought I was pretty smart after all that I had done during her convalescence. Mom always smiled and let me think big if it made me feel good about myself. At that time, we were living in Elkhart, Indiana. Daddy and Mom had heard of some beautiful property available in the rural area of the town of Middlebury, Indiana. They were tired of this moving around—they wanted to just buy some land, build a house on it, and settle down to take life a bit slower. At just eight-hundred dollars an acre, they thought that one of them should go over and take a look at it before making a final decision to buy.

On an extremely stifling, muggy morning, July 2, 1970, Daddy instructed Mom to take Herb and me with her at eleven o'clock for a drive over to see this property. And he made sure that we were to be back by three that afternoon. I protested that I didn't need to go, that it was hot, and I would remain with him. My remarks mildly irritated him, and he firmly said, "No. I said for the three of you to go on. Leave at eleven and be sure to be back by three."

With that being said, we left promptly at eleven; however, on the way we stopped at a dime store for some candy. There was an ominous feeling that started at the crown of my head and descended clear down to my toes. I told Herb that I thought we should go back home, but he insisted that we should carry out Daddy's instructions and look at the acre of land in question. On we went. But to go against a foreboding such as that has always troubled me. What would have been the outcome if we had gone back? I wonder.

Mom liked the property and the prospect of having a new home. She stood there looking at the acreage with the beautiful trees standing here and there. Her little face reflected her positive feelings about the land and the possibilities of the house that she and our daddy had in mind. Herb and I mostly thought of the room that we would have for a basketball hoop and our other sports interests.

Chapter Two **23**

We agreed that the property would suit our family needs just fine. I was beginning to feel a little nervous about our being late going back home, for Daddy had never before set such a time limit on any of our trips away from home.

Suddenly Mom started toward the car and motioned with her head for us to come on. It was time to go if we were to be home by three o'clock. As we entered the front door of our house, our little poodle, Petey, was acting very strangely. In fact, he was jumping up and down against the closed basement door. Another strange sight was how Daddy had placed his personal stuff along the edge of the bed in the master bedroom—his billfold, pocket change, the knife, a handkerchief, a bottle opener, and a little good-luck buckeye that he always carried. His shirt and pants were nicely hung on a hanger and were dangling from a wall light fixture.

How strange it all was. Eerie! Chills were beginning to form on the back of my neck. Where was Daddy?

How strange it all was. Eerie! Chills were beginning to form on the back of my neck. Where was Daddy? My next thought was that he was playing our little game of hide-and-seek, and if I found him he always gave me a fifty-cent piece of money. That's what I wanted to think when we got home. But I yelled in a loud voice, "Daddy, we're home! Where are you?" Deathly silence except for Petey's scratching on the basement door. At that point Mom went to the basement to look around for him. There were three rooms or areas in our basement: the laundry room, the pump room, and the root cellar that we referred to as "the potato room." We did, indeed, store our potatoes in dirt-filled boxes in that room high on wall-length shelves. That day only Mom went into the pump room and the laundry room.

She returned upstairs, and Herb came in from the garage with no news as to Daddy's whereabouts. I went back into my parents' bedroom to their closet, and the door was closed. I slowly opened it. Nothing. Then I went upstairs to my bedroom and stood in front of my closed, closet door dreading to open it. I didn't want to open it, because I was truly afraid that Daddy might be hanging there. I think the reason for my fright was the sudden picture in my mind of the effigies hanging around town after the KKK had been there for their practices. He was not in my closet, and Mom and I returned to the kitchen. Herb went downstairs and included the potato room in his search.

Just then the basement door flew open, and it was Herb. Never had I seen Herb like that. He was completely "white as a sheet" as they say, and his eyes were wildly staring at Mom and me. Herb apparently was in a state of shock. He was only sixteen, but he became a man at that moment. My heart has always gone out to Herb for the fact that he was the one to find Daddy that day. Instantly he protectively warned Mom, "Don't go down to the basement. I found Daddy in the potato room. Don't go down there, Mom! Please! Just call an ambulance!"

Herb was a large, muscular guy for his age, and he tried to block Mom from going to the basement again. Mom pushed Herb aside as if he was nothing and bounded down the stairs toward where she would find Daddy. Then I heard the most blood-curdling screams as Mom's voice echoed again and again from the concrete walls of the basement. It became wails and more wails and settled into moaning. Daddy was gone. The new house suddenly was forgotten forever. All that mattered at that moment was gone. The rug had just been pulled from under us.

I froze in place. "I'm only twelve. What has just happened today?" In a distant-sounding voice I heard Herb tell me to take Petey outside and tie him to a tree. In my daze and shock of the moment, I obediently took Petey out and tied him, but not before I went back into Daddy's room and found a cigarette in one of his dresser drawers. Recently I had sort of experimented with smoking.

It made me feel grown-up and "cool." I had just enough nicotine in my body to make me crave a cigarette in that stressful and overwhelming time and place. No one had ever warned me about the real dangers of smoking, so on I went toward that habit.

Back outside I went to peek out from behind the garage at the unfolding scene before me. It seemed surreal. I spotted a strange man near the vicinity of the front porch, and I went toward him spitting out some terrible words. "What are you doing here? Have you come to see a dead body?" This man must have been a friend of Daddy's because he left the yard in tears. Later I felt so ashamed of talking to this caring man in the way that I did. I never saw him again. Someone had called the police because I remember three or four squad cars parked around, and the policemen were going in and out of our house. Next came an ambulance. But, of course, last came the hearse. That put a finality on it all, but not before they heard from me.

I knew what had happened was true, but I was not ready to accept the reality of the situation. Remember, I was only twelve at that time and very much attached to this man that I called "Daddy." As I saw the hearse drive up, I came running out to the ambulance people to tell them that they could bring my daddy back, but we didn't need the hearse. These very compassionate people began to cry. Right then I turned to see some men rolling a gurney out of the house, and on it was my daddy who was covered with a bloody sheet. A big policeman was trying to hold me from going to the gurney, but in spite of his efforts to detain me, I broke away from this big man and ran over to the hearse. I took hold of the handle of the door hoping to keep them from opening it and placing my daddy inside. In the most powerful voice that I could find, I announced, "You are not going to put my daddy in this hearse!" And to the big policeman my words were: "You, Sir, are going to tell the ambulance drivers that they can bring my daddy back!"

This was a very delicate situation, and the authorities gave me a moment to vent my anger. Finally the big cop came over and gently pried my little fingers away from the door. All the while, he was softly talking to me and telling me that they had to do their job. I even went so far as to dismiss the hearse driver. I'm ashamed to say this, but I heard myself saying some choice words for which I later had to make apologies. Then the big policeman cradled me in his strong arms while I wailed and beat on his chest in my despair. "Oh, please! Please! Don't take my daddy away!" All hope faded as the funeral home personnel drove away with my daddy in their final care. I was one very angry girl.

First of all, I was mad at Daddy for doing this to me; mad, very mad at the ones taking him away; and mad at God for letting it happen. I realized later that even though my heart was breaking, God was patient with me to let me experience the well-known stages of grief, which I later learned that the first stage is anger. I was going to have to work through it, but it wasn't over and wouldn't be for some few years later on.

The thing with Daddy was that he had prophesied what had taken place that day, and I hadn't taken him seriously. I know now that when someone mentions suicide, this must not be taken lightly. The truth is, they have thought about it or they wouldn't be voicing it. That is the time to sit up and take notice and watch for the signs of impending action. Daddy sent us away on this day that he had chosen to end it all. Somehow I sensed it, but felt powerless as a young girl to take any action; after all, I had promised secrecy as you will see.

Daddy had been losing weight, and he couldn't seem to find the reason why. One day while he and I were out on the front porch, we had gotten into a conversation about cancer—probably because of Mom's having gone through so much in the recent past. Daddy went on to say that his mother had died from breast cancer. As an eleven-year-old boy and an only child, it had been his duty to change his mother's dressings. He remarked about how bad the odor was from the material on the bandages that he removed and changed.

Daddy startled me by saying, "If I ever thought that I had cancer I would kill myself." He even showed me the six bullets that he would put in his gun to do the job for him. I shuddered at the thought and told him in a pleading voice, "Daddy, don't ever do a thing like that! I love you. I need you." He turned me off by telling me not to tell anyone. I promised I wouldn't tell.

He just assumed that he had cancer and didn't want to go through the ordeal that two women that he dearly loved had experienced. So three of the silver bullets were fired. Bang! Bang! Bang! And Daddy was gone. The irony of it all was that the results of a recent blood test revealed that his weight loss could have been attributed to an abnormal thyroid.

> *Thunder, lightning, and a whirlwind were in this terrible storm that we were in, and its black clouds rained down salty tears that ran like rivulets across our scarred landscape. The tempest rolled in and over us.*

Daddy was born in Ireland, and on the day of his birth his own father went to the drugstore there to get a prescription filled for his wife (Joseph's mother). As he came out of the store, a Protestant sniper shot and killed his father, leaving his mother alone in the world with a newborn son. The Protestant/Catholic uprising was going on in that country at that time, and my grandfather happened to be in the way of a stray bullet. And he was gone.

Thunder, lightning, and a whirlwind were in this terrible storm that we were in, and its black clouds rained down salty tears that ran like rivulets across our scarred landscape. The tempest rolled in and over us. What else could there be? But more was yet to come. I dreaded the trip to "the potato room," but Grandpa and Grandma were waiting in their car for us, and it was time to go to their home for the night. Tomorrow would come soon enough.

Chapter Three

The Potato Room

There wasn't much sleep for any of us at Grandma's house that night. I would sleep a little and awake with a start as if in a dream. Did I dream the events of the day before, or were they real? Another short nap, and I was awake again. Morning came, and it was time for Mom and Herb to go over the dreaded details of final arrangements for Daddy; so, the two of them went to the funeral home. It was decided that Uncle Daniel and I would go back to our home to feed Petey. I told Uncle Daniel to go ahead with Petey and that I had some things to care for in the house.

I went in and stood in front of the basement door for a while in order to build up my nerves for the trip down the steps. I slowly opened the door, turned on the light, and tiptoed down first one step and then another. There were the usual strings of drying, red-hot peppers hanging from the ceiling, and on shelves below were Mom and Daddy's beautiful jars of food that they had "put up." I reached the bottom of the stairs, and I paused for a minute. The potato room was straight ahead. *Should I back out? Or should I go on and try to visualize my daddy's last moments? What were his last thoughts? Did he think about me and how I would feel at losing him? What about Mom and Herb? What about Patrick and the others?* I decided to go on toward the opening. There was no door to open into that area. I just went in. Nothing could have prepared me for what I saw. (Later, the mortician told me that every drop of Daddy's blood had drained from his body onto the potato room floor.)

> *I went in and stood in front of the basement door for a while in order to build up my nerves for the trip down the steps.*

Tears were pouring from my eyes, over my cheeks, and onto the floor where they were mixing with the red surface left there the day before. My whole body was shaking uncontrollably, and sobs filled the room as if they had come from the depths of the earth itself. Never had I seen so much blood, and I stood there wondering how much had Daddy suffered as he lay dying with his life-blood ebbing away. To think that he had made it through World War II without taking a bullet, and now this.

I could barely see through my tears, but somehow I found a rag and began trying to mop up the remains on the floor. In my cleaning efforts, I looked down and discovered Daddy's blood on my hands and feet. It may seem weird to some, but at that moment, I felt as if I was desecrating his blood by having it on me. What was I to do? I couldn't go back upstairs like that. I looked around and found an old shop rag and cleaned my feet. I went back upstairs for a shower, and then I felt terrible that some of Daddy's blood was being washed into the city sewer.

The funeral was to take place on July 4. Patrick, my brother who was a major in the United States Army, came home from Fort Knox, Kentucky. It was a sad time for him, too, since he and Daddy were so close. The viewing was the night of July 3, and overnight it turned stormy and cold for a 4th of July in Kentucky. There were even tornado watches in effect. Before the funeral could get started, Patrick was so overwrought with his grief that he had to make several trips to the men's room to upchuck. I felt so sorry for my brother.

There was a terrible scene that took place when a black friend of Daddy's showed up at the funeral home for the service. My step-brother, Roy, insulted this friend by saying, "You ("N" word), you get out of here. You don't belong here." I heard those remarks and found Patrick and told him what had happened. Looking back, I can see how emotions are raw at a time like that. Patrick found Roy and punched him hard for saying that to Daddy's friend. Patrick consoled the poor man, and he stayed by as the funeral began.

I didn't know the Lord at that time, so don't be too surprised when I tell you that I sounded off again at the graveside. I took hold of two of the casket handles, and again they had to pry my hands from them so that they could get on with their duties. The poor funeral director was again the recipient of a verbal bullet from me. I was so angry and frustrated. "First you took my daddy from our home, and now you (bad words) are going to put him in a wet, dark hole." I started sobbing again, and someone reached down and gathered me in their arms and tenderly placed me in the limousine for my trip back home. I don't remember who it was, but it must have been Patrick. We had done all that we could for our daddy.

At times, our daddy had come across as an earthy man. That was just part of his background and resulting personality. He had lived life with gusto considering the circumstances that thought to dismay him. His was an untimely demise and we were without an answer for it. In the military he had been privileged to travel the world. Now we had to lay his body to rest and try to make some sort of sense of it all. It was way too much for a young girl such as I to grasp.

My world had collapsed around me. *What was I to do?* I felt that I had been set adrift on an uncharted, turbulent sea which had signs of a squall appearing on the distant horizon, and I deliberately set my sails straight toward it. I wasn't going to be afraid. *I'm tough—I can handle anything!* Or so I thought.

(Years later after I had accepted Jesus as my personal Savior, I enrolled in a Bible college. One of the instructors was teaching on restitution, apologies, and restoration. He asked the class if anyone had anything that they needed to make right. Had they ever said words that they shouldn't have said? Guess what? The funeral director's face popped right up in front of my mind. I knew what I had to do.

I went back to Elkhart and found him in his office. I said, "You probably don't remember me." He replied, "Well, maybe I do." [Smile.] After he saw my two front teeth, he knew who I was. He was very kind, and he put his arms around my shoulders, and we both wept. "Yes. I remember you. You were the little girl who lost her father in the potato room in your basement. And the big policeman who held you in his arms, and unknown to you, had been in the potato room and knew what suffering you were going through. In fact, he quit the police department after that because the experience of seeing you so distraught touched his heart deeply, and he said that he just couldn't take it anymore.")

Chapter Four

The Safety Net

A pall spread over our house and everything once again seemed surreal. Our house became a two-week long, drunken binge for all its occupants who were left to mourn and cry. At that time, none of us knew the Lord, and I suppose we thought drinking would help soften the shock. The long, dark nights seemed to never end, and yet, I dreaded each day. Most of the time I kept to myself—sometimes weeping and sometimes spewing out words that I shouldn't even have known at my age. A frustrated and mixed-up kid would have been the description of me at that time. I sometimes wanted to just break out of the house and run and keep on running and running. Where would I have gone? But trouble was brewing inside of me.

Mom finally managed to hide her grief behind the sudden avalanche of papers to be signed. And the monument people became quite a nuisance for her. It seems that they descended on us immediately with each sales representative wanting to be ahead of the other. A monument was bought; however, I was too young to deal with that aspect of the tragedy. There were police reports, the death certificate, insurance papers, and social security benefits to consider since Herb and I were still minors.

One thing happened that I thought was so unnecessary. A young, rookie policeman was sent out for the final report, and because of his inexperience and lack of tact, he proceeded to tell Mom how Daddy had died. "Your husband went through a tragic death, and he suffered a lot before he died with pain and anguish. Three bullets were fired; one went through his neck; one lodged near his eyes; one went straight up." He went on to say that after they took the gun down to the station, that one of the cops tried to fire it and it jammed.

He didn't consider that I was standing there listening to his every word. It really upset me, and I ran upstairs to my room shaking all over and sending tears rolling once more. I don't know how my little mom could take all this considering the fact that her history included that long illness with cancer. But she held up, as they say, for Herb and me—although, I'm sure that in her private moments, she did a lot of grieving. How could I have known, as a child, that losing one's mate is such a devastating thing?

It was all about me at that time, and I was reacting in all the wrong ways.

Wild Child

It was not long after this that I started going completely wild. I was finally a teenager, had money from my social security check, and I began my plan of action. I was mad at God and mad at everyone in my path except for my new street friends—and they were mad, too! Daddy had taught me well. I could jump, and I could box my way out of danger with the karate moves that gave me so much courage in a fight. Then I decided to smoke myself to death on multiple packs of cigarettes each day. Yes, light one and the next one from that and on and on each day until fatigue took over. My stash of liquor kept me in a continuous state of intoxication, and I became totally out-of-control. On and on my anger drove me. Along the way drugs entered the picture. I found Daddy's sleeping pills, and on two occasions I took an entire bottle of pills. Obviously, the first stomach pumping didn't stop me.

> *It was not long after this that I started going completely wild.*

Mom threw up her hands in despair. She couldn't reason with me, and she finally gave up. For me, the questions were always: "Where was God? Why did He take my daddy?" Many nights the silent tears drenched my pillow. In spite of that fact, my attitude was, "No one would see me cry. I'll show them. It's me against the world." One can't go on forever without running down at some point.

Ice Ahead

One thing that slowed me down a bit was Christmas day that same year. My grandparents had come to Elkhart from Middlebury to spend the day with us. After they left, I noticed that two of their presents had been overlooked, and I suggested to Mom that we should take them to Grandpa and Grandma. We began our little drive, and as we started across a bridge, we hit a patch of ice. This caused Mom to swerve, and as she lost control, an on-coming car clipped us. This caused us to fly across the rail of the overpass to the dirt bank below. We somehow managed to miss a tree and a house, but, there was a parked eighteen-wheeler in our path, and we ended up under the monster.

The top of the car was laid back like a convertible when it hit the tire carrier located underneath the truck.

And in the speed of the moment, Mom almost suffered a complete scalping. It did lay her skull bare across the top of her head. I managed to squeeze out through a little window, but I received several cuts on my fingers from the broken glass. Amazingly, those were my only injuries. I had ducked down into the floorboard as we flew along. I soon realized that Mom was hurt and bleeding so much that her white fur coat was saturated with blood. I learned later that the scalp bleeds profusely.

At the sight of all that blood I started screaming for help, and someone called for an ambulance to take Mom to the emergency room at our local hospital. They treated her injury with an antiseptic solution, sutured the wound, and sent us on back home. I believe it was a miracle that we weren't killed that day. But God had other plans for us, and we were spared. The residual effect from that accident is a twitch that is still in Mom's left eye some thirty years later.

The old saying, "When it rains, it pours," seemed to apply to our family. It was one thing after another. We knew that my brother, Patrick, was stationed somewhere in Cambodia or in that region of the world. He was a major in the army, and he flew solo helicopter missions. That was about all we knew about his military duties. We got word one day that he was killed when his helicopter, which was loaded with guns and explosives, suddenly exploded in mid-air. We never knew exactly what happened, but we all experienced another round of grief and sorrow at the news of his death.

Betty Jo

My drinking and smoking continued. I was a very unhappy, bewildered little girl who was on a path to self-destruction. Something had to happen. You would have thought another death would have stopped me, but it didn't. One night a street friend of mine, Betty Jo, and I were having fun bowling at the local bowling alley. Suddenly she started going round and round the concrete pillar that was supporting the building. She began screaming, "Get those spiders off me; get those snakes away from me; get them away-y-y!" This scared me so much to hear her scream and then see her down on the floor butting her head against the concrete. Someone called for an ambulance, and another bowler suggested that I go to her and cradle her head in my lap to keep her from further injuring herself. I did what was suggested; yet, she continued to butt her head against me, and it hurt a lot. She was dying from an overdose of a mixture of LSD and alcohol. Thankfully I had never used that drug and never did, especially after seeing my friend die. She didn't make it to the hospital. She took in a breath, rolled her eyes back, let out that breath, and passed away right there in my lap. This caused me such sorrow and pain that I again reached for my solace—the liquor bottle.

Dry Tank

Finally, one night I sent myself into temporary oblivion. In fact, I don't remember how I got there or when, but I ended up in a dry tank surrounded by a group of men who were all in my condition. A dry tank is a circular room at the police station that is all enclosed with glass for police surveillance. I could have been dead for all I knew; however, God knew where I was, and at that time He chose to intervene in my behalf.

A New Daddy

Across town there was a mission headed by Pastor Amos Bauman and his wife, Mabel. Pastor and Mrs. Bauman looked after the physical needs of many homeless people as well as their spiritual needs. On the night that I was in the dry tank, one of the regular attendees at Pastor Bauman's mission Bible study was absent. Pastor Bauman sent another homeless man down to the police station to see if he could find the absent man—mostly to see if he was in any kind of trouble. The man that was sent saw me, a tiny, dirty little heap lying in the middle of a contaminated, concrete jail floor. It startled this man so much that he went back to the mission and informed Pastor Bauman of what he had just seen.

There I was, thirteen and alone with no identification on me. And there I was thirteen and suffering from a broken heart. I was tired, so tired! Skinny and emaciated little me had run down. Out there somewhere, a kind policeman had spotted me against a building or who knows where, and he had brought me down to the station. For the moment and for my safety, the police did what they had to do in placing me in that glass enclosure. I had come down to the bottom of the barrel, so to speak.

Pastor Bauman did, indeed, come down to the jail where he was well known for his benevolent endeavors around town. Many times the police called him in an hour of need. Well, I was given coffee in an attempt to sober me for the ride to the mission, and he and the police were bombarding me with questions. "Who are you?" "What is your name?" "Where do you live?" Their voices finally came into my consciousness, but they sounded far, far away.

Gradually, very gradually, I managed to open one eye and then the other. All this must have taken some time, but I wasn't aware of anything that made any sense to me. *Who was this man who was tenderly bending over me and speaking to me in such soft, caring tones? Where am I?* I was soon to find out who had come to spread the proverbial safety net over and around me. I was on my way to a place where I would find a balm for my healing in the loving care of Pastor and Mrs. Bauman. Drowsily I wondered what lay ahead.

Chapter Five

The Turnaround

You could say that Pastor Bauman was of a medium build; however, his wife, Mabel, was taller than he and "heavyset." He was at once kind, but firm in what he expected of those whom he served. Mabel was softer in her approach to any situation or person. They were a wonderful team that was mightily used by the Lord to alleviate the pain of any suffering humanity that came their way. That's what they faced in dealing with me—I was suffering, and they knew it. To pull out all the stops that they eventually did for me was a great show of Christ's love shining through them. I was to be a challenge that they would long remember.

First of all, I needed a real scrubbing, and Mabel took care of that for me. After that, I was given some clothes from the mission to wear. Then I was led into the kitchen where I was served a sandwich, a bowl of soup, and lots of coffee to sober me. With a bath and food in me I was more than willing to accept their offer of clean bedding and a clean cot for a good night's sleep.

For about the space of one month I was permitted to stay in the mission; however, this was a men's facility, and I wasn't allowed to enter their space. I was given a nook in the staff area, and I was allowed to use the bathroom there for my personal hygiene and needs. The personnel back there were very kind to me as I endeavored to find my way back to reality. School hadn't yet begun, and I needed this time to collect my senses. And I had some valuable lessons to learn and some bad habits and ways to unlearn.

> *I had some valuable lessons to learn and some bad habits and ways to unlearn.*

Where Was Mom?

(You may wonder about my mom. The truth is that she had to give up on me, for, you see, she had to work, and when she came home from work she would find me passed out from the alcohol. I was an alcoholic by then. Later in my life Mom apologized over and over, but I told her that she was helpless, and I was beyond her help as a mom. The experts had to take over that for her.)

After a month or so at the mission, Pastor Bauman thought that he could trust me enough to transfer me to what was known as the "Community House." This was an all-female facility where abused or battered women could find refuge, and sometimes for women who were suffering from tragedies such as losing everything in a house fire. Then I came along to be rescued. (Later I came to know one of the residents who had, indeed, lost her husband, her children, and their home to a fire.)

The House Rules

As we were going down the driveway to this house, I asked Pastor Bauman, "Do you live here?"

His reply was, "Yes, you and Mama will be the only women here today. And no outside males are allowed. It's just me as your court-appointed guardian for the time being."

Once inside he showed me around the downstairs; then he gave me permission to go upstairs and take the nicest room up there. I was puzzled—all five bedrooms were beautifully furnished. He came up and chose what he considered to be the nicest one, the end one which had a walk-in closet. For all these bedrooms there was only one bath, and I knew that meant there would be no time in there to fritter away in getting ready for school. A needed lesson for me was that I should consider others at all times even in small matters.

As I ascended the stairs he had remarked, "Unpack your stuff and come back down because we are going to have family time." I thought, *What is that? Family time?* Back downstairs I was confronted by Pastor Bauman who was holding a piece of paper in his hand with the title being "DENA'S HOUSE RULES." (By this time he had started calling me "Dena." And I began addressing him as "Daddy" and Mabel as "Mama." At other times, when speaking with someone else, I just called him "Dad Bauman.") At first I thought that house rules would be okay as he read the following:

> Five minutes per week allowed on the phone. *(And I was on a timer.)*
> No smoking or drinking on premises. *(Okay, I'm in his house.)*
> Only smoking allowed at the firehouse. *(And he should never see me smoke.)*
> No cursing anywhere—he better never hear me. *(Oh, me.)*
> You will be in school every day with no excuses. *(Really?)*
> Meals three times daily at 7:00 a.m., noon, and 6:00 p.m. promptly. *(I was to be there.)*

> Get up at 5:30 a.m., get them up at 6:00 a.m., have breakfast stuff out for Mama. *(Am I in bootcamp?)*
>
> After school a snack and upstairs for homework. In house by 9:00 p.m. for bed. *(oh, me. I'll be going to bed with the chickens.)*

Then Daddy concluded the list by announcing, "I expect complete compliance from you, and furthermore, you will go to church every Sunday morning, Sunday night, and attend prayer meeting every Wednesday night."

THAT DID IT!!! I exploded in anger when he told me that I had to be in church. My defiant chin went up, and my head went from side to side. "Who do you think you are giving me these rules. I've been on my own—no rules! I am my own boss! To (bad word) with you!" (I am so ashamed of all this, but I kept on with a few more sentences that I don't care to reveal. To think that this man and his wife had rescued me, cared for me, were still caring for me, and I had the nerve to address him in this way. And another thing that makes me sad is the fact that my own father taught me these words by his own example. I thought I was being cool and clever and so grown-up. That is not so. Satan causes his subjects to spout out such garbage.)

Chapter Five **51**

Dad Bauman knew that children need boundaries as to the kind of behavior that is acceptable. My behavior and words were definitely not okay in society, and he meant to teach me and show me my boundaries. Before I could react, I felt a pull on my right earlobe. "Come with me, young lady," and into the master bedroom we went. As we went by the dresser he reached for Mama Bauman's hair brush. Over his knee I went, and with me crying and yelling, I received the hardest whipping I had ever experienced. He didn't stop until I went limp. I had met my match. Don't feel sorry for me because that licking with that brush was long overdue, and I desperately needed to find a boundary. I had found it.

To say that this punishment was the last one that I ever needed would not be the correct assumption. No one is perfect after one correction; sometimes, it takes dozens more. Furthermore, after each one that I received I grew into a more promising human being. Looking back, I think I came across as a caged animal snarling and growling my way in life. I learned quickly to respect and obey these people who loved me enough to take time with me and see some potential good in me.

Sometimes I regressed and lapsed back into some old ways. My big problem was truancy. I know that my grief was at the heart of this problem; however, the rule was that I was to be in school. The truant officer would find me, and, in my case, his job was also to report this problem to the court. I became well known downtown at court. After about two years in the Bauman home, and my skipping school, we once again had to appear in court before the judge and give an account to him. I knew that everyone, including me, dreaded seeing him. He was known to "throw the book" at people.

Facing the Judge

After going over my misdemeanors, the judge just sat and glowered at me for what seemed like an eternity. In that moment I could feel his disgust from his years of experience at looking at others just like me. Then, as he squared his shoulders, he looked straight at me over his reading glasses perched way down on his extra-long nose. (Finally, I was at the point where I would sort of take notice as to what people would say to me and how they looked.)

The judge began, "Frankly, you mean no more to me than this piece of paper on my desk that goes into the trash can. You are worthless, and you will never amount to anything." I saw Dad Bauman flinch. Then to Dad Bauman he seriously began talking. "Frankly, Mr. Bauman, I don't know why you want this girl in your house! I wouldn't want her in my house."

Dad Bauman knew the judge very well, and he asked for permission to step forward in my behalf. "Your Honor, Sir. I believe this girl has potential. Please let me take her back to The Community House for one more trial period. I can't bear to give up on her. If it will please the court, I would like to see what else can be done in her behalf." The judge looked at Dad Bauman for a few minutes, and then he stood to his feet. With great reluctance, he gave Dad Bauman permission to take me back, and quickly, very quickly, he went to his chambers, but not without giving me his one last look of disdain and contempt. In that moment I felt like a garbage heap.

Frankly, you mean no more to me than this piece of paper on my desk that goes into the trash can. You are worthless, and you will never amount to anything.

We left the court with my crying and sobbing—the judge's words had cut me to the core. I saw myself as I was for the first time, and I didn't like what I saw. God was giving me conviction of my sins and wrongdoing. My heart was melting fast. When we got back to the house I was still weeping. I even asked Daddy, "What makes you tick?" I had seen Daddy accidentally hit his thumbnail with a hammer, and all that he said was, "Praise the Lord, anyhow. Glory to God." He didn't go into cursing and swearing that I had witnessed so many times with other people. And I had seen Mama Bauman, after burning two cherry pies, saying not much of anything. At that point, I told Daddy that I wanted what he and Mama had.

To my question of "What makes you tick?" he replied with his hand on his chest, "It's Jesus in my heart." Then he asked me if I was serious about accepting Jesus in my heart.

I said, "Yes! Yes!" At that point I was sent upstairs to my room to get a piece of paper and instructed to write down all my sins. At the top of the paper he wrote, "Dena's sins." I knelt down with Daddy beside me. I started writing down my sins as I thought of them, and then we began praying. Through my tears, I started confessing to God all my sins that I could think of. There were so many. If I hesitated, Daddy would say, "What else?" With my face to the floor, I cried and spilled out more confessions until I was totally spent confessing sins and began confessing Jesus as my personal Savior. I was a born-again Christian! I felt that peace come into my heart, and I became one changed girl on June 11, 1973. Praise the Lord!

(As I later learned as an adult and as a lady truck driver with my husband beside me, that a turnaround is just that. It is a place to turn around and head in the right direction. My place, my turnaround, was with Dad and Mama Bauman. That is where I did my turning around. I was now going toward the "right way." I was happily at the beginning of that road, but a few more signposts would guide me on and on. I didn't know it then, but I needed time for a more in-depth study into God's Word for my spiritual growth and development. I had met my Savior and Guide who would go with me on the rest of my journey.)

Chapter Six

Brand New

I had accepted Jesus as my Savior, and I felt altogether like a new person. I have since thought of that scripture in Isaiah 43:18 and first part of 19: "Remember ye not the former things, neither consider the things of old. 19. Behold, I will do a new thing...." And I was so thankful that John 3:16 included me. "For God so loved the world, that he gave his only begotten Son, that whosoever believeth in him should not perish, but have everlasting life."

I began to read and study my Bible that Dad Bauman gave me. Since my family had never given any thought to spiritual matters in my childhood, this was all new and wonderful to me. Along the way, at my request, I asked to know what the Baumans "believed." In the Mennonite church organization, they don't go into a serious Bible study with prospective members, but explain the plan of salvation and some lifestyle expectations from their members. It sounded okay to me, and I asked for baptism and church membership. One of the elders in the church doubted my sincerity, and he suggested that I should be given a trial period to prove myself. Eventually I was baptized (poured) on December 23, 1973.

The Sabbath?

Dad Bauman's Mennonite church that he pastored was called "The Lighthouse" and was located in Goshen, Indiana. I came to know and love the members there. They kept Sunday; I kept Sunday. The only time that I had ever heard any other day of worship mentioned was one day when I was around eight. My friend and I were playing in the front yard, and he taunted me with a statement. "Ha! Ha! Ha! Berdie, you don't even know which day is the Sabbath."

At that I was puzzled, and I ran to my grandfather who was working in the yard. "Grandpa, what day is the Sabbath?" To that question he cautioned me to go no further with it. I didn't know what it was all about—Grandpa was a nominal member of the Roman Catholic Church, and I now feel sure that he knew the answer but was afraid to say it. I simply put it out of my mind—but a tiny seed was planted. As I look back I know that God had a plan for my life that He was patiently developing.

Freedom

My truancy ended, and I continued living with the Baumans until 1976. My probation officer was so pleased with my progress—in fact, he was elated. The next time that I went back to court, another judge was presiding who was known for his leniency in judgment. He was very kind to me, and because of my good behavior and school attendance, my records at court were expunged never to haunt me again. I was a free girl, both socially and spiritually speaking. Freedom! What a wonderful gift from God.

> *My records at court were expunged never to haunt me again. I was a free girl, both socially and spiritually speaking.*

During my time with the Baumans, Dad Bauman felt that I should be given some in-depth counseling to prepare me for reception into society again. This was a daily thing, and it proved to be valuable in my preparation for adulthood. Before my conversion, I was sullen, angry, rebellious, foul-mouthed, and the list could go on and on. As I progressed through the Bible and Christian counseling, I became a happy, cheerful, cooperative, submissive Christian young lady. I found joy in going out on street-witnessing missions to see people give their hearts and lives to Jesus. Dad Bauman had me give my testimony hundreds of times. I was a changed person, and I found new life in serving the Lord.

In Transition

I stayed with Dad and Mama Bauman until the eleventh grade. Grandpa needed help on his farm in Middlebury, and he sent for me to come and help. Grandpa laid out his work plan for me by saying, "I'm going to teach you how to work. I always expect 100% from all my other workers; on the other hand, from you, Berdine, I expect 120%." He was tough, but I learned how to drive and handle a tractor, fix it if there was a mechanical problem, and he also taught me how to do welding. All my family had converted to the Mennonite persuasion by then, so it was nice to be back at this time with my family of like faith; however, I missed my other family that I left behind in Goshen, Indiana.

The friends that I left at the school in Goshen were a happy group of kids. We played together, ate together, studied together, and I hated to leave them. The situation at the Middlebury school at that time was a different thing—these were city kids. I was from the country and dressed in a different way. Many times I was referred to as "a country bumpkin." That hurt because most high school students want to fit in and be accepted by their peers. I know that I wanted that for myself. My past was hard enough for me to deal with, so I desperately wanted to be friends with these "city slickers." In time a few became a little more friendly.

I had sort of knuckled down to finishing high school and was graduated in May 1977. High school graduations are wonderful events; however, young people can never know what the future holds for them. It is a time of looking back as well as a time for looking ahead. As I went to sleep that night, I couldn't help wondering about my future. I drifted off to dreamland asking the Lord to show me His will for my life. I continued working for my grandpa, and as I was always interested in motors, I decided that it would be fun to own a motorcycle, and I determined that one day I was going to get myself one.

Chapter Seven

Breaking Home Ties

Dad Bauman's dream for me after high school was Sharon Mennonite Bible Institute located in Harrisonville, Pennsylvania, and this meant that I would have to make the move there and live in the dorm if that could ever happen. For the time being, I had to put thoughts of Bible school back into the recesses of my mind. I needed to keep on working for Grandpa and putting money into savings until the day that I could leave the comfort of his protection. I lived at my maternal grandparents' home around ten years, and life on their farm was never dull. But the thought of going to Bible school was exhilarating! I loved being around people, and it would promise to be a fun time with educational benefits if I could ever just get there!

My daddy was gone—I had pretty much reached the point of coping with that. Yet, I was on my own as a young, adult woman to work and "keep body and soul together," as the saying goes. Before his death, he always stressed to me the importance of taking care of Mom, so I always had her in my sights and still do to this day. She and I don't always think alike—she is more conservative than I am. But that is okay! We can be different and still love and respect each other. I'm constantly dealing with my wild side—I talk a lot, and I stay in constant motion as some of my friends timidly tell me. But I'm just me. You remember how I was before I accepted Jesus as my Savior. Now I stay gloriously happy for most of the time. Apparently this is the personality that God gave me, and He expects me to be all that I can be for Him in this armor in which I move.

Mom and I and various relatives were all involved in church work. Sometimes we boxed up tracts to be delivered and handed out, and we did community service such as food boxes and helping the elderly and visiting nursing homes. My enjoyment was street ministry. I believe with my heart that God placed me in a type of wilderness at this time in my life where He could develop my understanding and learning, my coping skills, my people skills, and a commitment to Him from which I would never waver. During all this time, life had its side events that made a whole lot of memories for me.

Pigs?

We had no idea that raising pigs and eating them was frowned upon by God. I certainly didn't consider that they were created as scavengers to help keep the environment clean. I think perhaps more people need to visit a pig farm to see how filthy these animals really are. Maybe it's hard for some folks to imagine, but Leviticus eleven was never included in any sermon or health talk that I ever heard. We had a hog pen on Grandpa's farm, and you knew it by the stench coming at you on a hot, sticky, summer night. In fact, the whole neighborhood knew it, but they took it in stride as part of survival.

One day I received first-hand knowledge of the contents of the hog pen. I decided to go for a ride on my little horse, Jenny. As we went riding by the pen, suddenly Jenny caused me to dismount without my permission. For some reason she began to shake violently as we went by, and I flew off her back, face down into the awful black stuff in that pen. My glasses were caked front and back, and it's a wonder that I even found them because I was covered, and I couldn't see so well with the fetid material in my eyes. No matter that I had on a clean pair of white designer jeans that were bought with my carefully saved money. Somehow I climbed over the rail and stumbled to the backyard where I found a hose to at least wash off the mess before I went inside. I learned to stay away from that pig residence down the way. Phew!

Finally, a Motorcycle!

For some reason, I always had a fascination for motors and the "Vroom! Vroom! Vroom!" of the sound of them. Perhaps Daddy's influence played into my wanting a motorcycle. I don't know. But I wanted one. Motorcycles can be fun, and they can be dangerous. Depends. As you will see, I paid a terrible price just to own one. Certainly ground and concrete don't give an inch when one slams a motorcycle down. Silly me! I hadn't given that possibility a thought.

I knew just what I wanted for my first bike—a sapphire-blue one to match my birthstone color. A Honda 125cc captured my eye and my pocketbook, and I enjoyed it for a while; however, my ultimate goal was to own one just like the one that I remembered seeing in my childhood—a coral Honda 350cc. My dream had come true when I finally had enough cash saved for that honey of a bike. I enjoyed riding it, and sometimes I enjoyed just walking round and round the bike studying each detail.

Mine, all mine. I had worked hard to get that bike, and nothing was going to stop me from enjoying it.

Things were chugging along with my work on the farm just helping with whatever Grandpa needed. One day when everyone was busy, I decided to take my bike out for a spin. That turned out to be a very bad idea. It was a beautiful day with a clear blue dome of sky overhead—a perfect day for a cyclist. My helmet was on, I had on some old clothes and my boots, and with a light breeze blowing, I was on my way. *Perfect*. The state line was not far away from where we lived, and before I knew it, I had crossed over into the countryside of the state of Michigan. Not good, but I was there, and I decided to go exploring down a tree-lined back road which had just the right amount of curves to lean in to as I went zipping along.

I had worked hard to get that bike, and nothing was going to stop me from enjoying it.

I was already over an hour's time away from home, and I wasn't paying enough attention to my driving. I was just enjoying the ride and the scenery when suddenly I was flying through the air. Somehow I had hit a huge clod of dirt that had been dropped by a plow, and this caused the back end of the bike to go up. I landed hard on the ground below and laid open my right kneecap to one side. I managed to get up, straighten up my bike, get on, and travel the painful miles back into Indiana and home. When I got home, I hid my bike in the barn and hobbled into the house to get some ice and some ace bandages. I was trembling all over, and I suppose I was in shock. And how I did it, I don't know, but I climbed up the stairs to my room, took care of the knee with my limited knowledge of sterilization, placed an ace bandage around my leg from ankle to above my knee, and climbed into bed.

When my folks came in they just thought I was hibernating in my room reading or something, until a day later I heard some grumbling about my welding work falling behind. On the third day, with my leg black from hip to my ankle, I painfully struggled outside to try to begin my work. I had no crutches at that time, and Grandpa saw me wobbling along and inquired, "What's wrong with you?"

To which I feebly replied, "I turned over my motorcycle and hurt my knee!"

"You did what?"

"I hurt my knee!"

Silence.

Grandpa was good when he was good, but when he was mad, he was very mad! He was upset that I hadn't told him about all this. You see, when I first got the bike, I signed two papers stating that I wouldn't travel in unfamiliar territory. The other one was that I would tell someone where I was going. So Grandpa decided that I needed a good whipping for breaking my agreement, and proceeded to give me a spanking. It didn't matter that I was suffering from an injury, or that I was a grown girl by this time. After the whipping I was taken to the emergency room for treatment. Surgery for repair was unavoidable, and I was referred to a surgeon. That surgery was unsuccessful; therefore, seven more procedures were tried over a period of several years to follow.

To this day I occasionally hit my knee on a table leg or some obstacle, and it sends me into orbit, so to speak. It completely immobilizes me for about fifteen minutes until the pain subsides. One might compare it to bone-on-bone rubbing together. It just plain hurts when this happens. It is at times such as this that I long for Jesus to come back and take us to a place where there will be no more pain. And someday He will do just that for all of us. Praise the Lord!

My motorcycle days came to an end with the sale of my bike, but I learned that one should obey the rules—the rules of the home in which one lives. And I learned in another way that God expects us to obey Him just as we obey those in authority here on this earth. Farm work and the usual church duties continued. I was happy; yet, I wanted more. I was getting restless and needed to get on with something else. What would it be?

Chapter Eight

An Interesting Encounter

Saving money has never been a problem for me since I became a Christian. (I don't spend it anymore on alcohol and cigarettes.) I worked in Middlebury and also on Grandpa's farm and saved part of my paycheck each payday. Finally, I felt that I had enough savings to seriously consider moving to Harrisonville, Pennsylvania, for my enrollment in Sharon Mennonite Bible Institute. Grandpa seemed reluctant to see me leave, although he felt that I should go on with my formal education, and I said goodbye to the old and ventured out to the new. I was so happy and thrilled!

This was a peaceful time in my world. No more weary days on the farm where I felt like I was getting nowhere, like a dead-end street. I was more than ready to hit the books, make new friends, and do some serious missionary work for the Lord. I liked the Bible Institute.

My professors were very strict, and I needed that. I knew they had our best interests at heart, and from the start, I decided I would try to do my very best. It's amazing what a few years of adulthood and hard work will do for a young person.

I had no trouble making friends in this environment of learning and doing. The campus was beautiful with the green landscape surrounding the simplicity of the buildings. Pennsylvania is in itself very pretty, and I felt so blessed to have the privilege of attending a Christian school such as Sharon. As I look back, I remember the students in their modest apparel and innocent-looking faces and all so eager to learn. I'm sure some were there to seek a suitable mate; on the other hand, I was there to study and move on to a higher calling.

I was more than ready to hit the books, make new friends, and do some serious missionary work for the Lord.

As I think back over the years, I can remember an amusing incident that took place at Sharon. My roommate, Betty, and I got hungry one night around midnight. I looked at her, and she looked at me. I whispered, "Let's go!" We cautiously headed for the kitchen which was down on the ground floor, and there we crept around by the light from the street light outside.

Suddenly my "partner in crime" let out a muffled scream. She had tripped a mousetrap, and it had caught her big toe in its clutches. We turned on the light under the stove hood to check on her injury, and just then the door opened to reveal the school administrator standing there. I innocently exclaimed, "Oh, Sir, you should be in bed at this hour of the night." He had been out for a walk to see if all was in order around the school. When he saw the light in the kitchen, he thought there must be a prowler inside the building, so he came inside to check on his suspicions.

Fortunately and under the circumstances he was in a good mood, and we ended our foray for food by my making our administrator a peanut butter and jelly sandwich along with ours. With our hunger pangs and Betty's toe taken care of, we headed back to our room and back to sleep. What a night! (And no punishment!)

Back on the Streets

The first two years went by in a hurry with our studies in the Greek language and other difficult subjects. Next came the time to put theory into practice. Mennonite Christians live a strict lifestyle in deportment, dress, and religious endeavors, and it became my time to begin my training in street witnessing. One particular professor put me with Jeff, a timid young man, as my witnessing partner. The plan was for us to go house-to-house doing a simple survey. Afterwards, the person surveyed would sign the two survey sheets, and those we turned in as part of our assignment for that day. I remember how we debated on going down one road. I started it by saying, "Let's go down this road."

Jeff wasn't sure. "I don't know anything about this road."

"I don't either, but the Lord told me to go."

It seemed strange, but in the end we decided to go. I had prayed earlier, "Lord, show me where you want me to go." (Later I became definitely sure that we did the right thing in going, but that wouldn't be a for a few years.) There weren't many houses down that way—I believe it was more rural with farms and gardens. We went to the door of one isolated house whose grounds revealed a beautiful vegetable garden and lots of fruit trees. We knocked on the door and a gentleman came out on the porch.

"What can I do for you young people?"

We, of course, were a bit nervous. "Well, sir. We are students at the Sharon Bible Institute, and we are taking a survey in your community. Would you mind completing these few questions and sign your name for us to turn in as part of our assignment?" I looked at my friend who seemed a little nervous as he stood looking down. About that time the gentleman finished signing the papers and handed them to me with these words:

"What day do you go to church?"

"Sunday."

"My dear child, you don't know what day to worship on?"

I was dumbfounded. "Huh?"

I cut my eyes over Jeff's way. He motioned that we should go.

Then this gentleman told me that he was a Seventh-day Adventist Christian. He went on to tell me briefly why Saturday was the Sabbath. He referred to Exodus 20: 8–11, and Genesis 2:1–3. I politely listened to him as he was telling me this new truth, but I began to back away as I listened. This was so new to me, and it sort of frightened me. I softly said, "Thank you," and tiptoed down the steps to catch up with Jeff, who had already walked on ahead. We didn't discuss this incident. Jeff just seemed to drown out the man's words; however, I thought and thought about all that he had told me.

The next day I asked Harry, the school administrator, "Why is it that we go to church on Sunday instead of Saturday?"

He lowered his eyes as he seemed irritated. "Whom did you talk to?"

I showed him the paper. "You are not to go to that house anymore. Do you understand that, Berdine?"

I pressed on. "Why *don't* we go to church on Saturday?"

"We're not to discuss this anymore."

"Well, okay!"

That was not the end of this for me. The Adventist man had been so kind to me, and I thought about it for a long, long time. Finally other things pushed this to the back of my mind where it would lie dormant for a few years only to be remembered and brought to life again.

The Back Stroke?

Along the way, we students were allowed freedom for a few sports and social activities. A young couple occasionally came to the services of the Mennonite church that we attended. We girls learned that they had a swimming pool, and we longed for an invitation to come to their house to enjoy the pool. As a Mennonite, I knew that our beliefs included "no mixed bathing"—girls with girls, and boys with boys. (Years later, I still feel strongly that way about this issue, and I wish other Christians could see how this indirectly affects the morals of society.)

One week this couple invited the girls over for some fun and games around and in their swimming pool. I didn't know how to dive, and one of the girls knew that, but she proceeded to dare me to dive off the diving board. I protested. She kept on daring me, and I gave in and stood on the end of the diving board just waiting. Suddenly I jumped up and off, and as I started down into the water, I arched my back in a wrong way and broke one of my vertebrae in my fall. This caused me much pain and discomfort as I struggled with school work in my recuperation period. And learning to walk with crutches was not easy, either. The lesson for me in this was that wrong choices, no matter what pressure you are experiencing, have their consequences. I thought a lot about that.

Graduation

Time was moving on toward my graduation day. As an incentive, Grandpa had offered me a trip to Israel if I kept my grades to a B-plus; I ended school with an A-minus, and I had done well in my Greek studies. He was so proud of me, and so was my mom. The promised trip to Israel was with a group, and we had a tour guide who had been our Bible instructor. He knew Bible history so well, and he made it all come alive once we arrived there.

For our trek around the country, we had secured the services of a tour company before ever leaving the United States. There were several of us young people on the tour, and our bus driver noticed the deportment of these friends of mine. There was no scuffling around, no hand holding, no kissing on the bus, and this driver was puzzled. I told him that was how it was with our group—that we didn't hold hands until we were engaged to someone. He seemed amazed. I must have "struck his fancy" because he asked me to marry him and be his wife number four. I laughed and told him, "We don't believe in having multiple wives." And besides, I wouldn't have been attracted to him. I had long before then decided that when and if I married, it would have to be to a Christian man.

I had given my testimony so many, many times over the years, so I suppose it was natural for them to ask me once again to give my testimony to the people in the conference room at our hotel. Each time that I endeavor to do this, I try to reach the other young people in attendance with the importance of, first of all, giving their hearts to Jesus. Always it follows that I want to show them the evils of alcohol, cigarettes, drugs, profanity, and indifference to societal norms.

I was anxious to get back to the states and give an account of this most important trip of a lifetime. To think that I, a little Indiana farm girl, could go to the Holy Land and experience the thrill of being where Jesus walked. Nothing could ever top this; yet, I was eager to see what the next adventure would be.

Chapter Nine

Mistaken Identity

In my community of faith, I was what one would call a conservative … all the way conservative which included lifestyle, dress, style of worship—the "whole nine yards." It never offended me for others to stare at me, laugh at me, or disagree with me. From my past you could say that I still retained some attitude which at times was a good thing. Mom had adopted my new faith a few years prior to these events that I am about to share.

My great-uncle Ernest enjoyed singing in a barbershop quartet group. Uncle Ernest decided that he and his wife, Dorothy, would fly out to Salt Lake City for a singing convention being held in the convention center there. Barber shoppers were going to be there from all over the United States, and he didn't want to miss this one. He also graciously purchased tickets for Mom and me to go, too, if we wanted to. We had to furnish our transportation and expenses—he just provided the tickets for the five-day event.

I was around twenty-eight by this time. I had been working in town and also on my grandfather's farm, so I had enough cash saved for a nice trip like this. I was more than eager to get started. My problem was a rattletrap, '82 coupe GXB210, five-speed Datsun for the trip, but I was sure, (hoping) that it would get us there. We washed and polished the old, dull-brown car as if it was a Cadillac sitting out there in our driveway. I surely didn't want to offend my old vehicle by driving into Salt Lake City with Indiana dirt all over it. It didn't seem to matter that the floorboard was mostly rusted out, as they say.

In my community of faith, I was what one would call a conservative ... all the way conservative which included lifestyle, dress, style of worship—the "whole nine yards."

We had made it into Wyoming on I-80 when I heard a whole lot of rattling going on underneath my feet. I pulled over, got out in the rain, and peered under the car. Something was hanging down under there. No problem.

I just reached into my toolbox and pulled out one of Grandfather's long-handled pliers and crawled under to take care of the matter. I cut loose the piece of rusted floorboard, crawled out, stood up, and was showing Mom what I had done when suddenly I heard the horn on a big rig as it went sailing by. I must have been a sight standing there in my unique dress, stockings, hair style, and to top it off, I was holding a pair of pliers in my hand. I'm sure the other truckers along the way heard about that strange sight on the interstate.

On we went to Salt Lake City. Now the only problem was that I could see the pavement going by under my feet, and I had to sit with my knees together and feet apart as Carol Burnette used to do on her television show. (Get the picture?) To add to that dilemma, Mom sat over there scared to death that I was somehow going to get hurt.

In our Mennonite faith, the women wore no adornments, no make-up, and no frills. Our clothes for the trip consisted of solid blue dresses whose hems must touch mid-calf. The necklines were simply bound with bias strips, and a cape was sewn into the dresses for our unique style. Stockings were dark, and shoes must be black and of the study kind. (In other words, ugly.) My hair was midway down my back, but I had to wind it into a bun at the nape of my neck. Away from home my head was always covered with an eyelet cap of sorts. Mom's hair was shoulder length, but always in the covered bun. This is how we presented ourselves at the convention.

Did we ever stand out! Other ladies were wearing the latest designer styles, nice slacks and tops, and evening wear at night. Not us. We had on our plain blue dresses and held our heads high! Did we get noticed, and how! People were opening doors for us, smiling at us, and watching our every move. One day we walked over to the hotel where our relatives were staying and sat down on a bench in front of a beautiful fountain to wait for them to meet us there. People were coming to us and asking permission to take our picture, and we said, "Sure, go ahead." Others were exclaiming, "They're here! They're here!" We were blinded by all the flashes.

Mom looked at me in bewilderment. "What's going on?" (I was enjoying all the attention.)

"I don't know and have no idea, but I don't mind this at all." I was all smiles and flirting with the cameras. When we went to a restaurant, people would pick up the tab for Mom and me. My poor uncle couldn't figure out why he wasn't in on all our sudden popularity.

One day we met up with them again at their hotel, and he tried to hail a taxi. No luck. I said, "Let me try it." I stepped out and put up my hand and whistled. Three or four taxis pulled in to the curb with the drivers arguing who should get us. When I saw their problem, I said, "Let me choose." The driver that I chose was an Asian gentleman. We wanted to go where we had parked our car; however, he wanted to take us on a tour of Salt Lake City. He insisted, so on we went, and it was very beautiful. The Wasatch Mountains were magnificent as they towered toward the sky on the distant horizon. We also thought the great, Mormon Temple was an architectural masterpiece—the spires were striking. (Someone told me later that the angel high above the temple represents the Angel Moroni.) Our driver was excited to be taking us on the drive around the city. "How do you like Salt Lake City?" he asked with his Asian accent. We assured him that we were well pleased with our trip here and there around town.

Finally, he took us back to our hotel where we got our car. We needed to go to a drugstore for an item, but there and everywhere we went we were shown such respect. Mom and I knew very little about the significance of Salt Lake City to a large number of people. We just went there for the convention and got caught up in some sort of excitement about our appearance. We were from a small town in Indiana and members of another set of beliefs, so, what did we know?!

The next day was scheduled for our trip to the tabernacle downtown. One of the guides accidentally touched my arm. "Oh, I'm so sorry that I touched you." I told him not to worry, that I was only human. I wondered why he apologized for touching my arm. We were escorted to the platform where the huge organ sat, and I reached out and softly stroked a corner of it. To our guide that spot that I touched became a special untouchable spot for anyone else after that. I had touched the organ.

Mom and I started to cross at an intersection, and the old knee injury "acted up" suddenly, causing me to stop in horrific pain in the middle of a busy crosswalk. The lights changed two or three times; no one blew a horn, and no one moved. At the third light change, two or three men came from their cars to help me cross on over to the other side. Such nice people in that city! Mom and I still couldn't figure out what was going on.

At our hotel, the maids wanted any hair that I pulled from my comb and placed in the trash can. It was the same for our toenail or fingernail clippings. (I am not kidding.) One couple gave up their room for us and even paid for our five-nights' stay. Mom and I thought that the windows of heaven had surely opened for us in that city. Never mind the old Datsun.

Uncle Ernest and Aunt Dorothy were flying back to Indiana, but before they left Uncle Ernest rigged a floorboard for me, and it was something to behold! But, it did at least put my feet back into a more comfortable position for driving. We arrived back home in Indiana after another two weeks traveling and sightseeing. In the mail was a letter from Uncle Ernest, and in it was a page from a Salt Lake City newspaper with the heading: "THE TEMPLE LADIES HAVE ARRIVED," And underneath that heading there appeared to be a picture of Mom and me sitting on that bench with the hotel fountain behind us.

Pikes Peak

I have always loved our beautiful western states since childhood; however, a sad event happened that has forever stayed in my memory. In 1964 our family was privileged to tour parts of the West that included the famous Pikes Peak. It was late spring, and there were patches of ice in certain shady spots along the way to the top of the mountain. As children, Herb and I enjoyed this side trip up the steep incline, and at the top we found other children who became instant friends. I remember that we talked with some girls and a boy who had come with their parents that day. The wind was blowing, and it was quite cold for that time of the year. Mom had provided jackets for us, and we reached for them as we got out of the car.

After an hour or so of enjoying the view and searching for souvenirs in the gift shop, Mom decided that it was time to leave. We told our new friends "goodbye" and we got into our car. We started on down the mountain, curve after curve, when suddenly a car came flying around us, apparently speeding for the current conditions of the road. The adults in our car later wondered if his brakes had gotten hot.

At the next curve we witnessed what was an awful moment in time. The children that we had met and played with were at the back window screaming as their car went off the side of the mountain. Grandpa, who happened to be driving, managed to sop our car for us to see where these people were. My grandma and Mom crawled over as far as they dared go because the road had "given way" at that point. It was deathly quiet, and their car was nowhere to be seen. When Mom and Grandma got up to come back to the car, more of the roadbed started to break. The adults surmised that this driver hit that spot where the road had crumbled, and over they went. They had completely disappeared. We found a ranger and told him what happened, and he said, "We won't be going looking for them. They are gone."

I've never forgotten that incident nor the faces of those children as they went over the edge of that thousand-foot-plus drop.

Chapter Ten

Jail Houses Again

In Mennonite circles I became well known because of my testimony concerning my conversion. People who don't know the Lord need to hear how God can change lives. I know He did a great work in my life, and I appreciate His sacrifice on Calvary to make eternal life possible for me, and the whole world, if they will only come to Him repenting.

Dad Bauman frequently had me tell my story at his Faith Mission.

People who don't know the Lord need to hear how God can change lives.

I didn't mind, and I've always made myself available if it will help someone else. Looking back at this long interval in my life, it seems that the thrust of Mennonite missionary endeavors is to tell as many people as possible about the plan of salvation and then give them the opportunity to accept Christ. To join their church one only needed to express a desire to become a member solely on just being born again. To sit down with someone and have them study lengthy Bible lessons was not part of their church style. Mennonites are very nice and wonderful people, but they have been deprived of knowing so much more about the hidden things in their Bibles.

This was how I was taught as a teenager, and that was my style. I continued helping at Dad Bauman's when I happened to be in their area. Then I received an invitation to minister to the inmates in a city facility for men in Michigan City, Indiana. This is where I ministered for some time before accepting an invitation to minister to maximum-security women inmates in the prison in Centerville, Michigan. This jail ministry meant a lot of moving around for me. I became friends with Sheriff Matt who made me the assistant chaplain for the prison in LaGrange, Indiana. You may wonder how I made my living—I wasn't proud, so I worked as a dishwasher at night, and I did my jail ministry in the mornings. I did this for several years.

As I said before, I became well known in Mennonite circles such as missions, jail ministries, and as a speaker at our camp meetings. This led to an invitation to go to Los Angeles, California, to help with the work there. From there, I and others went to Mexico where we ministered in several villages. The hospitality that was extended to us was unbelievable. It goes without saying that we enjoyed the tacos, the beans, and the other delicious Mexican fare that was offered to us. Next on my itinerary was Chicago, Illinois, for more witnessing programs such as jails, streets, and churches.

About Mom

Mom was in and out of my life during these years. Sometimes we shared a house or an apartment, and sometimes I lived alone while doing whatever was asked of me. Finally, I set my sails for the West by moving to the beautiful, Grand Canyon State of Arizona. Mom came out in 1996, and we have been mostly together all these years. She is a great mother! She has had her share of sorrow and heartbreak; still, she manages to "hang in there." She is loyal to me, and I value her very much.

About Herb

Herb was always a hard worker even as a teenager. After our father's death, Herb stepped up to help Mom all that he could. He worked for a gentleman down the way from our house. As an adult, Herb lives in Arkansas and works with a worldwide, delivery service. He is a devoted brother, and I love and appreciate him as he encourages me every step of the way. I'm very proud of him as my brother.

Arizona

My reason for moving to Arizona was to become a teacher in the Mennonite school located near the city of Phoenix. It was a good move on my part—I liked the people and I liked my position. The children were fine young people who made my life easy as a teacher. However, I am saddened as I look back and think about how things changed at the church and school there. The pastor was controlling and tried to interfere even in my private life. He was constantly pointing out my flaws that he perceived needed correction. I felt like it was plain harassment, and I chose to leave that fellowship once and for all. (Looking back, I believe God was directing me in this choice.) I'm sorry about the need that some had to rule others. It's okay to be a leader who is kind and caring about its members, but it is another thing to constantly try to intimidate the laity. I truly believe that God was moving me along toward His ultimate plan for my life.

I started having feelings of not being able to "measure up" to the strictness of the rules imposed on me by my so-called superiors. Constantly I was made aware of what I should do and what I shouldn't do. A red truck was a "no, no." My clothes were being scrutinized; even my conversations were picked apart as to what to say or not to say. No one can hold up for long under circumstances such as these. I simply exited the front door never to return. I left behind some friends that I hated to lose; anyhow, it was time for me to move on and think things through for a while. Ten years were what I needed to make some sort of transition to something else. Little did I know when I left that church what would transpire on down the road ... *the right road.*

Chapter Eleven

High Noon

Learning new things is a joy for me. Since it was mostly me against the world, I always looked for ways to increase my income so that I could do missionary work when asked. Over the years I completed my certified nursing assistant studies plus some advanced study in that same field. This led to several positions in the medical field where there were openings—medical assistant, phlebotomist, laboratory assistant, and general floor duties. Perhaps you could call me a "Medical Jack-of-all Trades." Anyway, I tried to do my best.

After I left the Mennonite group in Arizona, I began to lose weight at the rate of 5–6 pounds weekly. Having been around medical work I knew that wasn't good, and after finding a lump myself, I made an appointment with an oncologist. You must remember that Mom had cancer early in my life which made me wonder about myself.

The oncologist scheduled my surgery for a biopsy and a radical mastectomy if the biopsy was positive, and I signed papers to that effect. I was nervous as you can imagine. He went on to say that even if the biopsy should be negative, that he would go ahead and do a lumpectomy, which would remove just the tumor rather than a mastectomy.

Another thing that had happened was that I was occasionally attending an independent Baptist church in the little town of Congress, Arizona. I liked the interim minister and his sermons very much. (And he was handsome!) When he learned that I was in the hospital and the reason, he came to my room and asked if he could anoint me and pray for my healing. Such a sweet, sincere prayer was offered in my behalf, and as he concluded with the "Amen," I seemed to have a feeling in my chest like hot liquid was moving out of the area. I even said, "Well, I've never felt anything like that." We both started believing for my healing.

Surgery was the next morning; the biopsy was negative! The mastectomy was not needed! I was healed! Praise the Lord! As I said, the surgeon went ahead as planned and performed the lumpectomy; however, this meant a few days in the hospital, but I wasn't complaining. If you have never had the big "C" word spoken over you, then you might not understand my obvious exuberance. But if you have, you will understand my joy and relief. Life had stopped for the moment; now, life could resume.

Herman Gehring, the minister who prayed for me and visited me in the hospital, became my best friend. He is a man of integrity, and I treasured our friendship because I felt that he was honest and true. He served in the military in The United States Navy, and he did, indeed, travel around the world, so to speak. He and his deceased wife were parents to a beautiful set of children who matured into beautiful adults. Herman's goal was to tell as many people as possible about Jesus and how He came to this earth to seek and to save lost mankind and to reveal the Father's love.

Herman had completed a two-year theology course at a Bible college in Atlanta, Georgia. He was a soft-spoken speaker, which I liked. Since we were good friends, we shared many times together over dinner, walking in the desert, and climbing the mountains in our world. (We're still hikers.) This wonderful friendship deepened into mutual love and respect. We both knew where we were heading; on the other hand, we each had some bills and obligations that needed to be finished before we could ever consider anything more than friendship.

Finally, one day Herman said, "Berdie, I need to talk to you. Could we just go for a walk out in the desert where it is quiet and talk?" I agreed to that suggestion because the desert is such a quiet and serene place for contemplation, However, it can be a hostile place if one isn't following the rules. As seasoned desert hikers we knew just how far we could go and when to turn back. We also knew to watch for wildlife such as javelinas, scorpions, rattlesnakes, and Gila monsters, and we knew that these critters come alive when it gets cooler and darker in the day. We surely didn't want to interrupt this time together in a battle with one of them.

Some of you, especially the ladies, will wonder what I wore on this occasion. For our special walk that day, I chose to wear an outfit which I think Herman had given me. It was an embellished shirt that I paired with designer jeans that I had bought on a rare shopping trip to Phoenix or somewhere in the area. He complimented me on how nice I looked. As usual he wore his idea of western wear with the cowboy shirt, jeans, boots, and of course, the black felt hat. Perhaps we looked like a couple from some western clothing store advertisement. I don't know. It didn't matter to us—we were together, and that was enough.

As we were walking for at least a half mile on that bright, sunny, Arizona late afternoon, we spoke of the beauty of the plants there such as the giant saguaros, the thorny chollas, and the slender ocotillos. And it went without saying that we each loved horses and dogs.

We knew that God was in the way that we met, how God had led in our lives thus far, and how He would guide us if we kept trusting Him. We always seemed to go back to the truth about God in each of our lives. The contrasting colors of the rocks and the beauty of the plants all seemed to set just the right mood in the glow of the moment for that memorable day-of-all-days. The sunsets are beautiful in Arizona because of all the dust. On this day the sun was starting to get low on the western horizon, and the rocks were reflecting that special light at that magical time of the day.

> *The anticipation of the moment was almost more than I could contain. My heart was racing wildly, and I couldn't stop it.*

I knew that Herman was preparing to say something that would include the two of us. The anticipation of the moment was almost more than I could contain. My heart was racing wildly, and I couldn't stop it. I had never felt so much like this was somehow likened to something very spiritual and something very beautiful. After a long talk about this and that, we turned back and arrived at Herman's truck. My heart seemed to skip a beat in anticipation of what he really had on his mind. He spent a few seconds just looking down into my eyes. I caught my breath as he asked me one of life's important questions.

"Berdie, I love you so very much! Will you marry me?"

It didn't take me but a second to reply. "Yes, Herman, I will marry you! I love you, too!"

This may surprise you, but we had never even held hands during those approximately two years of our friendship. After the proposal of marriage, we joined our hands together for that first kiss of our love. Then he tenderly enfolded me into his embrace as he whispered his words of love and endearment to me. There has never been anything to equal that moment of all moments for any couple who find themselves in love with each other. It seemed that suddenly time stood still, and that we were the only ones under God's blue dome above. We felt that God's blessings rested on us as we began making plans for our lives to be joined together, and we made sure that we made Him first in those plans. Our engagement present to the other was a watch. We are practical people—we each needed a watch, and that is what we decided would be our engagement gifts.

The Wedding Day

"High Noon" is a popular time for weddings in Arizona. (You know, the shootout at the O. K. Corral, and the other legends of the West. Thank Hollywood for that.) High noon. The wedding ceremony was to be performed by the justice of the peace in Yarnell, Arizona. A lot of my friends were in attendance for the wedding and for the party afterwards. And, as you can guess, the table was loaded with all the traditional food items—cowboy beans, barbecue potato wedges, zippy coleslaw, and of course a wedding cake and ice cream for dessert—plus some steaks that were grilled outside. (It was wintertime, so no one had to stand by the grill with a rifle to watch for rattlesnakes.) Herman and I were attired in western clothes, boots and all, for our wedding, and we had specified that same theme for our friends who were horse lovers as we were. The day after Christmas, 2001, we became Mr. and Mrs. Herman Gehring—wedding ring and all.

It's Snowing!

Herman and I were truck drivers for a company in Phoenix, Arizona. We drove as a husband-wife team for several years, and during that period we had incidents happen where we knew that God and His angels intervened in our behalf. I remember well the time that we were on I-40 just outside of Flagstaff, Arizona. It was snowing, and before we knew it, it was snowing so hard

Chapter Eleven **99**

that we entered what is known as a "whiteout." Believe it or not, we were blinded.

Suddenly the barely visible outline of the back of a tractor/trailer came in sight, and we were going to slam right into it. Herman yelled, "Pray!" I called out, "Lord, forgive me of my sins. I'm coming home!" I closed my eyes in what I thought was the inevitability of the situation. We were traveling in the left lane of traffic, and at that moment, Herman left the road toward the median strip, we went into a dip, and our rig went on by the other one. No wreck! No crash! We both knew there had been divine intervention in play at that moment. We had been blessed and spared. We had a prayer of thanksgiving right then and there—for us and for the other guy.

I can remember the time that I was driving through northern Arizona with Herman asleep in the bunk above, and again, snow was falling. In the wintertime one can expect lots of snow in that part of the world. As I have told you before, I like to meet challenges if there is a faint possibility that I can win, so I decided to keep on driving. As it happens, I attracted a caravan of cars behind me, and in many of them was a scared woman at the wheel. None of these drivers thought to pass me because they were grateful that I was up front leading them through some deep snow. When we got through that part of the mountains, they each in turn passed me and waved a hand of thanks as they went by. I tooted the horn back at them as we went on our separate ways to our destinations.

Another time that stands out in my memory is the time that Herman and I were driving along a highway in the Norfolk, Virginia, area. Ahead of us we noticed a wall of rain coming right at us. For sure, we took notice rather quickly—I said, "Lord, we need a parking space. Please provide just the right one." Ahead was a truck stop, and we pulled into a beautiful space that meant that the wind and rain would hit our truck and trailer at just the right angle. We grabbed a few things and ran for the building, but we were drenched from the skin out. Can you imagine our shock, and at the same time our relief, when we discovered that *Hurricane Faye* was going up the coast in her fury and devastation.

We stayed put in the building for the night. The next morning, we got the all clear to proceed cautiously onward. When we got out to our rig, there was a huge barrel lodged halfway under the trailer, and one of the mirrors was pressed against the side of the tractor. That mirror was replaced at a price tag of under fifty dollars. No big deal—we had found "shelter in the time of storm," as the song goes, and our damages were minimal. And on we went still trusting in the Lord always for our safety.

I Am Praying for You

Herman and I strongly believed in prayer, and with the perils of the road you can understand why. We sometimes prayed for residents of the many houses that we passed on our journeying, but this time we included some cows. One bright, cloudless day as we traveled across Texas, we drove by a huge pasture on our left that was occupied by a large number of beef cattle. I looked at Herman and said, "Let's pray for the owner of these cattle that he will prosper through them." Herman prayed, and then I prayed this prayer for prosperity for this rancher way down in Texas. Sometime later we happened to be traveling through that part of the state again, and many of the cows were obviously expecting. This was a time for us to be joyful for the owner. We said another prayer and kept on traveling.

Our itinerary was such that we again happened to go back by that very same ranch only to see yearling calves scampering around and between the adults. Some were still nursing. We were almost squealing in delight at that point, and the rancher never knew that someone was praying for him. It makes one wonder who might be out there praying in our behalf.

What Happened to the Big, Blue House?

I feel that I would like to share one other story that stands out in our minds with regard to prayer for others. Sometimes we traveled northeast into the middle American states. Many times we chose US Highway 54 which could be very scenic in places on this route. One particular time we got on this highway in Tucumcari, New Mexico, and headed out for points along this route on our way home to Congress, Arizona. We had been on this highway many times, and in Greensburg, Kansas, there was a big, blue house, and we had actually prayed for the people who lived or worked there. The house was so unusual that it naturally got our attention.

When we got to Greensburg that last time a policeman stopped us at the edge of town. We looked around, and the town was flattened just like a war zone. We asked the gentleman what had happened to the big, blue house that stood over the way from us. He said that a huge, supercell tornado had roared through the town the night before, leaving behind the destruction that we came upon that morning and which included the blue house. It was gone!

One lady came over to our rig crying in desperation that she had lost her family and all of her possessions, house and all. By this time Herman and I were also crying with these people. The storm was one-and-a-half miles wide which destroyed everything in its path, including eleven people who lost their lives, and physically injured seventy others. It was determined that this particular tornado was an EF5 category storm, which is the worst that can be documented. The roads were such that we had to have a police escort to lead us on through their town and on toward home. Needless to say, we were shaken by the experience. That day in Greensburg, Kansas, May 4, 2007, can be researched on the computer with a pictorial and aerial account of the event.

During our driving days, Herman and I covered the highways and byways of our beautiful country. We encountered thunderstorms with fierce lightning; we drove through rain, hail, wind, and snow, but most of the time through sunny days. We can never know how many times our lives were saved—I'm sure there were many. This is a beautiful land, this land that we call America. As never before I appreciate our country and all that it stands for here, and how it is known around the world. I wouldn't take anything for our journey, and perhaps we would still be driving if some health problems hadn't forced us to leave that work for our recuperation. But before that retirement, a momentous thing happened that has forever changed our lives.

Chapter Twelve

Looking for a Church

Ten years can go by in a hurry when a lot is going on in one's life. After leaving the Mennonite church, I was never a permanent part of any church that I attended. That is not to say that I didn't enjoy friendship and fellowship of the members—I did. I made many, many friends along the way who have been a blessing to me, but something was missing, and I didn't know what it was. We began to feel that what was missing was church fellowship in something that was more Bible based. We felt that we needed an anchor-point.

Sometimes we were "on the road" for twenty-eight days without coming in home for a rest. Mom was living with us in Congress, Arizona, and as we neared home from any of these long trips, we only had to call her and gourmet food was promised when we got there. It didn't matter if it was in the dead of night, she always responded to our call. Usually we were so tired and so glad to come in for a respite from the grind of the road. I don't know how we could have made it without my mom waiting there at home for us. She was always faithful to our needs.

One spring day around four o'clock, we came rolling in toward the ranch in Congress. We were very anxious to get home, but before we could get home, we stopped in for our mail at the Wickenburg, Arizona, post office. We piled our mail in the truck and drove on to our ranch home in Congress where Mom had a delicious meal waiting for us. *Home*. Such a precious word! We were tired and weary and so very glad to be back in our home. Our wonderful, rescued dog was, as usual, doing his best to tell us that he was happy for us to be back. That long tail was wagging, and he was jumping up to our shoulders for joy at our being there.

(Before I go on, I want to tell you about Cheyenne, our dog who was thrown into a cactus plant by a cruel person. He was rescued by the police and taken to a veterinarian, who removed dozens of cactus needles from his little body. After his recovery, we were chosen and blessed to take him home with us to become our beloved pet. Many vet visits later, and given much love by Herman and me, Cheyenne was transformed into a beautiful canine.)

After our meal, I went ahead in for my shower. As I dressed, Herman was opening our mail. As he opened the mail, he came across a brochure advertising some meetings at an auditorium location in Wickenburg, Arizona. He stood up and announced, "Berdie, we're going to that meeting tonight. It speaks of Daniel and Revelation. I want to see what it is all about. Let's go." We both were weary from our travels, but suddenly we felt energized as we started dressing for that meeting that night.

When we arrived, the people were already going in. I looked at Herman. "Let's go, 'Baby-Cakes!'" As we walked in, a white-haired gentleman came toward us with an out-stretched hand of welcome. I immediately felt drawn to him, and for some reason, before I could even think about it, I blurted out, "We're looking for a church!"

Can you imagine his reply? Without missing a beat, he said, "You have found it!" That's what he said! The people were very kind to us as they smiled and shook our hands. And I well remember the atmosphere in that place that night. It was wonderful! There was an anticipation of what was about to be presented, and when the lights were lowered, Herman and I were ready to receive whatever the Lord had for us.

I remember the message on *"Unlocking Revelation"* and how Herman and I were so impressed with the truth of the subject and the clarity with which the evangelist spoke. (The white-haired greeter was the evangelist, too—Pastor/Evangelist George Garrick.) For the next few nights, we found ourselves on the edge of our seats as we sat on the second row of that church auditorium. As we left each night, the evangelist would ask, "Will we see you next time?"

We nodded, "Yes!"

We had planned to leave again in a few days for another twenty-eight days on the road. Herman and I simply shut down the truck after the third night of the meetings because of what we were hearing and learning. It was all so new and wonderful; we didn't want to miss anything. Inevitably we had to go on another trip, but not without contact with Pastor Garrick, who called us frequently to see how we were doing. Especially did he call us each Friday night around sundown.

Herman and I simply shut down the truck after the third night of the meetings because of what we were hearing and learning. It was all so new and wonderful; we didn't want to miss anything.

This new interest gave us extra energy and anticipation of going home for the next few meetings. One wonderful feature was the fact that the presentations were being taped. That meant that we could "catch up" on the ones that we missed. It also meant that Mom was watching programs via these DVDs and making decisions for each truth that she was also learning.

The Dreams

I might mention that the pastor's wife, Charlotte, played piano for these meetings. Each night when we were seated, she always turned and smiled a greeting to us. Bonding with her was easy, too, because we felt Christ's love reaching out to us through this caring couple.

The significance of Charlotte's playing was the fact that she had to help her left hand with the on and off button on her electric piano. Because of a torn rotator cuff, her left shoulder had "locked," and she was unable to reach the button with her left hand without help. In an earlier time, I had a dream which depicted what I saw when a blond-haired lady turned the on and off button on her piano, and it caused chills to see Charlotte do this same maneuver. (Her hair was also blond.) I wondered if this was the end of my dream.

Again, I earlier had dreamed of a large one-story house which had a multitude of doors throughout the house. During all of this time of attending these meetings, Herman and I were invited to the pastor's house for a meal. Charlotte took us through the house to show us the layout of the rooms. To my amazement, there were multiple doors all over their home. Again, that dream caused me to stop and think when I went through these doors. It all looked so familiar to me from my dream. Could this be from the Lord to let us know that we were where we should be on our journey to finding the right road?

Through Pastor Garrick we were given a correct biblical understanding of end-time events: the visible second-coming of Jesus according to John 14:1–3, Matthew 24, Acts 1:9–11, and more. The state of the dead, as found in one of many scriptures such as John 11:11–14, was presented. We studied the Sabbath truth of Genesis 2:1–3, Exodus 20:8–11, John 14:15, Revelation 12:17, 14:12, 22:14, 1 John 2:4, 5:2. What I came to realize was the fact that Jesus kept the Sabbath. That was especially brought out in Luke 4:16 ("as his custom was, he went into the synagogue on the sabbath day, and stood up for to read") and other places. (These KJV scriptures were recommended for our study, among others.)

The Sanctuary was an interesting subject which we studied in Exodus and Leviticus and other places.

We discovered new insights out of the prophecies in Daniel, the three angels' messages, biblical baptism, and so many more subjects.

One thing was discussed that intrigued me, and that was the study into healthful living. My and Herman's diet wasn't the best since we were on the road quite a bit, and I thought nothing at ordering a ham sandwich or a pepperoni pizza. Um-m-m! It was a shock to read Leviticus, chapter eleven, and discover that shellfish were off the list of good foods. I didn't know that eating shellfish could cause cases of the flesh-eating bacteria that is becoming more common these days and can kill its victims. Never mind buzzard or mouse, but it went on to say that pork (swine) was on the forbidden food list according to God's Word.

It took a little time of transition for us to take all that in and make new decisions. It was pointed out to us that our bodies are the temple of the Holy Spirit, and that alone helped us make the right decisions. It was impressed upon our minds, too, that eating the right foods doesn't save us. Salvation was stressed as we knew through what our Savior did at Calvary. I sat and took notes each night, and we went home and looked up the texts again. We studied the Bible thoroughly and the truth-filled literature that we were given for more information into each subject.

The more we learned, the more we were amazed at all these new revelations out of God's Word.

If you remember, when I joined the Mennonite church, I was not immersed in water—they simply poured water over my head. That was quite an eye-opener for me when I learned how it really was supposed to be according to the Bible. Herman had already been baptized; however, he chose to be re-baptized since he had learned new Bible facts. In these meetings we learned so many beautiful truths, and we knew that we had some serious decisions to make. As we traveled up and down our nation's highways, we spent more and more time studying our Bibles, reading spiritual literature, and praying more. And we had lots of time in our discussions.

> *We studied the Bible thoroughly and the truth-filled literature that we were given for more information into each subject. The more we learned, the more we were amazed at all these new revelations out of God's Word.*

"I'm convinced, Herman, as to what we should do."

"Well, Berdie, I need to think about the Sabbath change a little more. That is not what I was taught at the Bible college in Georgia. I'm not sure the day is that important," "And listen, Herman, remember the Sabbath was given at Creation, written on that table of stone by God's finger. And another thing, dear, Jesus kept it, and according to Isaiah 66, we will keep it in the new earth. What more do you want? And Jesus was there at Creation when the Sabbath was given if you remember that scripture that we studied in Colossians 1:15, 16. We love the Lord, and I want us to follow Him all the way without a ten percent discount."

"I know, Berdie. But let me ponder that a little longer before I come to a decision."

"Okay, Mr. Herman. By the way, are you going to read your Amazing Facts lesson this afternoon?"

And he answered so sweetly, "Yes, dear."

In one of the hand-out literature papers given each night after the presentation, was a Sabbath lesson from Amazing Facts. Getting more insight from this source helped Herman with his final decision for the Sabbath and for baptism with me. When we learned about the Sabbath and that it was from sunset on Friday evening to sunset on Saturday evening, we started parking our truck along the way and began worshiping the Lord during that special

Chapter Twelve **115**

time each week. This was so new; yet, we felt so blessed in observing this day as the Bible says in Exodus 20:8–11.

Pastor Garrick relayed two stories to us which involved his own decisions about the Sabbath some years before. He said that back in the fifties he and his dad had gone to an evangelistic presentation on the study of the Sabbath as it is given in the Bible. He said that after hearing that new revelation, he went to his pastor and asked him what day is the Sabbath. The pastor stalled by saying that we keep Sunday because of the resurrection. After being pushed for a definite answer, he reluctantly answered, "Saturday is the true Bible Sabbath."

The second incident was when the evangelist's father asked him to go to the local Catholic priest and ask him what day is the Sabbath. The evangelist said that when he was a young teenager that he had mowed the grass in the yard of the priest's residence, and so he knew him. As the evangelist explained, he went to the priest and asked him, "What day is the Sabbath?"

To that question the priest said, "Saturday is the true biblical Sabbath."

And another question was, "Who changed the day from Saturday to Sunday?"

Without any hesitation on his part, the older priest said, "We did. The Catholic church did. You will find that on page fifty of the convert's catechism."

Then the evangelist asked him, "Well, if I want to keep holy the Sabbath day, which church should I attend?"

The following was the priest's answer: "Well, if you want to keep the Sabbath and worship at the church that worships on that day, I recommend that you go out to Chestnut Street, turn right on Main Street, and turn left on Henderson Street. At the bottom of the hill on the right is a Seventh-day Adventist Church. They are the nearest to the Bible of any Protestant denomination out there. That is where you should go, young man."

Those two stories helped shape our life-changing decisions that we would make. We both agreed that the priest was honest about the answer.

As I told you, Mom listened to every one of the DVDs that we brought home, and she loved them and agreed with every truth presented on them. On the first visit from Pastor Garrick to our home, she ran to him, threw her arms around him, half crying and half laughing, and exclaimed, "All you are saying is true!"

We began some home studies with the pastor that helped the three of us make a final decision for baptism. How could we not make a decision while knowing and reading what the Bible said about every doctrine that was presented to us? We carefully weighed every one of the doctrines, and with the Bible behind each one, we knew in our hearts that God was calling us out for a new walk with Him. We felt an inner peace that was beyond anything we had ever experienced.

Pastor Garrick wisely left three baptismal bags for us to fill with a towel and a necessary clothing change for our upcoming special day of all days. August 15, 2009, was the day the three of us went down into the Wickenburg, Arizona, Seventh-day Adventist Church's baptismal pool for our baptism. It was one of the happiest days of our lives. Finally, we were home! Finally, we had found the right road that always pointed us to Jesus, The Way! Our search was over.

Finally, we were home! Finally, we had found the right road that always pointed us to Jesus.

Epilogue

Earlier in my story I told you how that harsh judge pronounced me as "no more than a piece of paper to be thrown in the trash can" and that I "would never amount to anything." Finally, he was proven wrong. God had me in His plans all along—it just took a while for the right timing in my life's journey. God knew me before I was even conceived, and He had me in His sights all along. I know this is true from what it says in Psalm 139:13–18, especially verse 16:

> *"Thine eyes did see my substance, yet being unperfect; and in thy book all my members were written, which in continuance were fashioned, when as yet there was none of them."*

It wasn't too long after our baptism that Herman and I were on the platform at the Wickenburg Seventh-day Adventist Church as part of their worship team. Sometime later, we were asked by the church board, in vote, to become elders. And wonder of wonders! I eventually became "head elder." I felt honored to be placed in that position in God's house; however, I also felt unworthy. It was a privilege and honor that I took very seriously.

At this time in my life, I appreciate my husband and friend, Herman, more than ever. In 2011, I almost lost him when he suddenly became ill with a huge blood clot that extended down his left arm to his wrist. It was a life and death matter for a day or two, but God saw fit to bring Herman through this ordeal. Today Herman and I walk on down life's road together, each striving to do the Lord's will and work wherever we can.

Mom moved with us to North Carolina, and she is very happy in this greenest of green state. She lives in a quiet cove near the many foothills scattered about in this region, which is a few miles south of the famous Grandfather Mountain. She loves the Lord and continues to be a great blessing in our lives. These days I am more than happy in serving the Lord in any way that I'm asked to serve. I look around in my little sphere of living, and the signs point to the Second Coming of Jesus. As I look to points around the world, I am almost mentally bombarded with signs. Just as Matthew 24 states: "Wars and rumors of wars, pestilences, earthquakes, fire, wind (tornadoes), men lovers of pleasure more than lovers of God" (author's words). It is time to seek the Lord; it is time to win others to Him, and it is a time to "Watch."

Even though I finished my course at the Sharon Mennonite Bible Institute, I felt that I had hardly scratched the surface of biblical studies when I started learning new truths and methods in the Adventist church. Pastor Ron Halvorsen did lay pastoral training seminars around the country, and soon after my baptism, he came to the Arizona camp grounds for a seminar. Several of us from Wickenburg went there for a four-session time of instruction. Pastor Garrick was in charge of assisting Pastor Halvorsen; therefore, Herman and I were also invited to be of assistance at these meetings. We finished the required four sessions and received our certification as "Lay Pastoral Assistants" or "Lay Pastors." We learned how to prepare sermons, how to visit people, how to get decisions, how to help young Christians, and numerous other things. Never had Herman and I been so happy in the Lord!

In 2013, Pastor George and Charlotte decided to move back to their native state of North Carolina, and go into semi-retirement. Quitting entirely from the Lord's service was never in their minds. Since they had relatives in the Piedmont section of the state and three daughters and their families in the Asheville area, they decided to move to the little town of Lenoir, North Carolina. Lenoir is approximately half-way between the two areas, which would make it convenient for visiting each other.

Because of some health problems, Herman and I were off the road by this time, and we were free to drive one of their vehicles across country for them when they moved to Lenoir in April of 2013. Since I was so susceptible to heat strokes in the hot, summer temperatures in Arizona, my doctor advised me to move to a cooler climate. When we got to North Carolina and experienced the mild temperatures in the foothills there, we decided that we also should go ahead and move to Lenoir. We have never regretted our move; in fact, we feel sure that we are just where the Lord would have us live.

At this writing, Herman and I and the Garricks are planning an outreach in the nearby community of Hudson, North Carolina. Our desire is to minister to the people in this little town for whatever their spiritual needs might be. In addition to that aspect of our goals, we plan health talks, budget-planning seminars, Red Cross training in CPR, etc. Because of the love of music expressed by so many in that area, a gospel singing is also in the planning. Certainly we want any of our efforts to glorify the name of Jesus. In the future, a prophecy seminar will be conducted by Pastor Garrick which includes a beautiful slide program.

Everything that happened to me was the Lord permitting it to happen as polishing stones and stepping stones through life. I must admit that it was tough at times. My Companion on my journey toward the right road has been Jesus, the Way. Always He was just a step ahead, urging me on and upward—especially since I gave my heart and life to Him on that night with Dad Bauman so long ago. Someday we'll "pull in home," and the troubles of the road will seem as nothing. When we get to the portals of heaven God will welcome us into His everlasting dwelling place, sons and daughters forever His. Praise the Lord forever!

Psalm 139: 23, 24, says, "Search me, O God, and know my heart: try me, and know my thoughts: And see if there be any wicked way in me, and lead me in the way everlasting" (KJV).

TEACH Services, Inc.
P U B L I S H I N G
www.TEACHServices.com • (800) 367-1844

We invite you to view the complete
selection of titles we publish at:
www.TEACHServices.com

We encourage you to write us
with your thoughts about this,
or any other book we publish at:
info@TEACHServices.com

TEACH Services' titles may be purchased in
bulk quantities for educational, fund-raising,
business, or promotional use.
bulksales@TEACHServices.com

Finally, if you are interested in seeing
your own book in print, please contact us at:
publishing@TEACHServices.com

We are happy to review your manuscript at no charge.

www.ingramcontent.com/pod-product-compliance
Lightning Source LLC
Chambersburg PA
CBHW070543170426
43200CB00011B/2529